Copyright © 2021 by Live To Produce Publishing Group

The 4 C's

Creating Change for a Better Tomorrow Starts Today

By Dr. Anana Phifer-Derilhomme

Printed in the United States of America.

All rights reserved under International Copyright Law. Contents and/or cover may not be reproduced in whole or part in any form without the express written consent of the writer.

ISBN: 978-1-952963-09-4

Live To Produce Publishing Group Mesa, AZ 85212

FOREWORD

Dr. Anana Phifer-Derilhomme is one of the most influential leading voices for young women in the areas of diplomacy and humanitarian work that I have personally seen with my own eyes around the globe. Her work to develop and create the 4Cs Philosophy has impacted young women from different countries and put them on the global stage as voices to impact and compete for their future.

This book is a philosophy and an action plan that Dr. Anana Phifer-Derilhomme created to help aid the world in global change. She has empowered young women as authors, to create and write new narratives on how to solve global issues in a post COVID world. As you read the 4Cs you will be inspired and empowered to be a part of the rebuilding of the Global family. You will be introduced to the voice of the future. The world is in great hands, because of amazing young female role models that have decided to take their future in their own hands and move the global needle forward. Dr. Anana, this is needed in this day we are living in. You are continuing to make people better every day. As the leader of the new Philosophy of the 4Cs, you are truly making the world a better place.

Sir Clyde Rivers
World Civility Leader

INTERNATIONAL RECOGNITION

This book is a necessary platform that exposes and showcases the brilliance of girls from around the world. I applaud you Dr. Anana Phifer-Derilhomme for your courage to deliberately harness their sagacity to provide insight that would inform us in the new dispensation. The 4C's philosophy during a post COVID-19 era, captures our imagination to envision the possibilities of advancing our humanity. You and I both are being mentored by the great Sir Clyde Rivers and I remember when you first visited my country, Guyana as a part of a team. However, as a result of your passion to cultivate the wisdom of girls motivated you to return to conduct your amazing BlessedGirls program. My nation is grateful for the impact of your program, so I know for sure that this philosophy is tested and proven. I thank you for your sacrifice and commitment to transform our future with the 4C's philosophy.

Dr. Astell Collins BD1
Better Defined One Leadership

TABLE OF CONTENTS

INTRODUCTION 1

CHAPTER ONE: CIVILITY MORE THAN A QUICK FIX 5

CHAPTER TWO: COMMUNITY STARTS THE MOMENT YOU'RE BORN 17

CHAPTER THREE: CIVILIST ON THE RISE 31

CHAPTER FOUR: CIVILITY BEGINS WITH ONE INDIVIDUAL 51

CHAPTER FIVE: COMMUNITY KINGDOM CONNECTIONS 63

CHAPTER SIX: COMMUNITY REQUIRES COMMUNICATION 73

CHAPTER SEVEN: CREATIVITY: EXPLORING NEW IDEAS 85

CHAPTER EIGHT: DARE TO BE CREATIVE 91

CHAPTER NINE: DON'T BE ORDINARY, BE EXTRAORDINARY 97

CHAPTER TEN: CHANNEL YOUR INNER CREATIVITY .. 111

CHAPTER ELEVEN: BURUNDI FACES THE EFFECTS OF CLIMATE CHANGE 127

CHAPTER TWELVE: CLIMATE CHANGE: OUR CRITICAL ASSIGNMENT 133

INTRODUCTION

The 4Cs Philosophy encourages reflection and action. This book encompasses our current standing and encourages us to take action now for positive changes that will impact our future. You've heard it said, "the future is female." This book features females today that will impact the future. 4Cs: Creating Change for a Better Tomorrow Starts Today is a book that is leading the way in Female Dialogue & Diplomacy.

The world needs this book. The world needs to hear the voices of women and girls because the Future is Female. As you continue to read you will understand why the statement is true. The future demands equality. I am confident that the young women who have contributed to this book will profoundly contribute to their communities and create the change we want to see in the world.

The females are watching, learning and preparing now for the future. These young ladies and women are experiencing life, they are facing challenges, and they are offering solutions. Solutions to some of the major issues we are facing as a people, as a country, as human beings. Each of these young ladies come from different backgrounds. Our youngest author is only 14 years old. At 14 years old she has a perspective, a vision, and advice for all who will listen.

As the Women and Youth Civility Practitioner & Global Ambassador for iChange Nations, I have traveled the world; I have worked with women and girls of all ages, races and ethnicities. The one common thread that is missing or lacking is civility. Civility is necessary to build a strong, healthy, progressive community.

The 4C's

Civility is necessary to promote creativity and ingenuity. Civility is necessary in recognizing and establishing ways to mitigate climate change. Civility leads the way for justice. We can all participate in Social Justice and Climate Justice and Restorative Justice.

The 4Cs is about taking responsibility. Take responsibility for where you are and where you are going. Each of the authors are taking the opportunity to independently be the change agents in their community. The 4Cs will give you permission to think independently and use your voice to change the world. You have the power. Power is your ability to act or produce an effect. When you utilize your power you tap into your influence and become the authority, just as our authors have. You can create change in your community. You have the ability to tap into your creative mind and find solutions. A closed mind restricts access to the various possibilities. As you read, open your mind to possibilities, opportunities and partnerships that can create the change you want to see to create a better tomorrow.

Each of the Cs are areas you can focus on independently or consider working on all 4 collectively. I advise you select 1 of the Cs that you are most passionate about and get to work. This book is for the doers. Those that want to see change but are not sure exactly how they can work to manifest change. After reading this book you will be able to start where you are and visualize improvements and advancements you'd like to see in your community.

As the founder of BlessedGirls, I have chosen these 4 pillars to uplift and support the work we do to empower girls and women. So consider the 4Cs as legs to a table. Each leg is important to the stability of the table. The table can hold your food, books, government, body, and anything else you place on it. The 4Cs help to support the table, which will provide a level surface on which objects may be placed or that can be used for such purposes as eating, writing, working, or playing games. The 4Cs provide opportunity for self-evaluation as well as cultural checkpoints to assess our capacity to listen, learn, and lead. Each chapter is unique, thought provoking, and purposeful. The purpose of this book is to stimulate your creativity and your innate ability to see the possibilities when we work together and consider our actions.

The fact is what you do today will have an effect on your tomorrow. How you treat your neighbor; how you communicate to your children; how we consider our recycling habits today all will shape the world we live in tomorrow. Our culture seems to forget the irony of this.

Mentoring girls and women, I have developed an ability to recognize opportunity, identify talent, and discern hurt. My name is Dr. Anana. I am passionate about empowering women and girls to become today's leaders. I have gathered women and youth leaders from around the globe to share some of the major issues facing our world today. The 4Cs are critical aspects we must consider, evaluate, impact, and improve in order to move forward and see a better tomorrow.

Bringing Women and Youth from around the globe to increase dialogue and bring civility for a brighter tomorrow. We want to provide a platform to dialogue and discover real solutions for the many challenges we are facing today.

Dr. Anana Phifer-Derilhomme is passionate about serving the community and creating opportunities for women and youth to be the catalyst for change.

The 4C's

CIVILITY

Civility comes from the Latin word civis which means citizen. I believe that it's our civic duty as citizens to be civil and look for ways to show kindness and understanding.

The opposite of civility is incivility, a general term for social behavior lacking in civility or good manners, rudeness or lack of respect for elders, vandalism and hooliganism, through public drunkenness and threatening behavior. How many of us have seen or experienced an increase in incivility lately?

Everyone wins when we embrace civility. I call them your Vitamin Cs It takes courage, consistency and confidence to create an environment where civility is the standard. Civility begets a oneness and a wholeness amongst people who appear to be of very different cultures, values and religions. Civility brings unity and solidarity. Begin with Civility to achieve success.

Dr. Anana

Chapter One

CIVILITY MORE THAN A QUICK FIX

Britney Valladares

Civility is a work of the imagination, for it is through the imagination that we render others sufficiently like ourselves for them to become subjects of tolerance and respect, if not always affection." - Benjamin Barber

I can remember after a long day of classes and training, I was wearing joggers and my dad's hoodie; my hair was a mess and I just didn't care how I looked, I just wanted to get home. As I was about to exit the compound I noticed a couple of girls my age studying every inch of my body, the disgust evident on their faces. I ignored them, pitying their narrow-mindedness, but part of me wanted to go over and yell "Boo!" just to make them uncomfortable, to do to them what they were trying to do to me; what they likely did to anyone who didn't fit their idea of what people should look like, especially a female of my age. That, however, was just one incident. The Golden Rule is the principle of treating others as one wants to be treated. I now turn and look at people when they're rude to me, not afraid to show them that they've hurt me just a little, and let them see that hurt, not the anger and ugliness that we so often put up in front of our pain.

The 4C's

Maybe their pain will see mine, and we'll recognize something in each other that reminds us that being a little kinder is the only rule we ever need to know.

Life can be hard, and people lash out. A lot of us are exposed to a lot of unpleasantness. I want to equip others with more than just enough to survive it; I want them to be able to see the good amidst the tough realities and help make the good stronger, but these are skills I'm still developing myself. Rude behavior sometimes overwhelms the general kindness that can also be found everywhere; one hostile comment or even a glare can undo the work of many quiet smiles, waves, or an unprompted greeting. I've traveled to a lot of places and met different kinds of people which caused me to encounter various forms of incivility. Building a civil culture means leaders must think beyond quick fixes. It's a marathon and not a sprint and, I believe, civility is the essential glue that holds society together.

Civility is about more than just politeness; although, politeness is a necessary first step. It is about disagreeing without disrespect; listening and seeking common ground as an initial point for dialogue when differences occur while, at the same time, recognizing that differences are enriching; listening past one's preconceptions and teaching others to do the same. Civility is the hard work of staying present even with those with whom we have deep-rooted and fierce disagreements. It is political in the sense that it is a necessary prerequisite for civic action. But it is political, too, in the sense that it is about negotiating interpersonal power such that everyone's voice is heard and nobody's is ignored. (*What is Civility? - The Institute for Civility in Government*)
https://www.instituteforcivility.org/who-we-are/what-is-civility/
Civility begins with us. Through positive, respectful communication

one person has the power to improve morale, productivity, and teamwork.

This past year has been trying for all of us. The reality of COVID-19 arriving on our shores is revealing the ugly side of humanity. Droves of people were panic buying and hoarding everything from toilet paper to canned goods, with scenes of chaos and selfishness playing out in every grocery store.

Compounding the confusion is the mixed messaging from our leaders and public health officials to stay home and practice social distancing, yet approving a broad definition of what is an essential business. The ongoing counts of infection rates and deaths combined with the states of emergency at different levels of government are leaving many of us in a state of perpetual stress.

Many workers are facing job losses or told to stay home with little direction on how they will pay the bills and feed their families or how long this will continue. Small business owners that have sunk their life savings into their businesses are having to close their doors, with little or no direction as to what lifeline governments can or will throw them. We are also seeing daily examples of profiteering and braggadocious behavior. Selling sanitizer at outrageous markups is certainly sleazy. And on our social media feeds, everyone is now a public health expert spreading meaningless, if not dangerous, advice and memes. *(Civility in the face of a pandemic | Brampton Focus) https://bramptonfocus.ca/civility-in-the-face-of-a-pandemic/*

Given our current environment, many are lamenting the lack of civility in today's society. A most prominent focus of this concern centers around politics. As I write this from Guyana the lack of civility in political discourse has reached toxic levels.

Unfortunately, this is not something that pertains only to Guyana. Whether it's the wrestling of votes or the increased debate about nationalism in countries around the world, people are claiming their positions and digging in. Aside from the lightning rod of politics, other topics (which are seemingly associated) are wearing down our civility and accelerating a societal divide. Entrenched positions tied to class, race, religion, gender, culture, and geography (i.e. urban/rural), to name a few, are solidifying a new tribalism. An "us" versus "them" mentality is emerging.

It is a foregone conclusion that the COVID-19 pandemic will cause untold deaths and impact world economies. As individuals we can choose to believe we have little control in the outcome of a global crisis and forget about civility. Or we can live with a renewed appreciation for our family members and neighbors. We can strengthen our social fabric by being better citizens and supporting the efforts of all those that are doing their part to get us through this.

We are seeing daily initiatives of people and businesses stepping up in Peel Region to help those less fortunate and isolated. These heroes are as important as our health professionals, researchers, grocery store clerks, truck drivers and first responders in the gratitude we owe. Let's not forget about teachers, professors, and students of all ages trying to carry on learning over online video solutions that leave much to be desired.

If we are to get through this crisis and be better as a consequence, we need to elevate our civility and social responsibility.

Despite the gloomy picture society has painted, it's reassuring to know there are small glimmers of hope out there. Emerging are organizations and thought leaders who are imploring a return to common decency, civility, and respectful exchange. This past

Christmas BlessedGirls and The Girl Build Girl Foundation, which focuses on the empowerment of young ladies, gave back to the community helping young ladies obtain certain essentials. These two organizations, among many others, are working tirelessly in giving back to the community, in giving to the youth, hoping that the kind gestures they leave behind are influential in bringing up a more civil generation.

"Civility does not ... mean the mere outward gentleness of speech cultivated for the occasion, but an inborn gentleness and desire to do the opponent good." - Mahatma Gandhi

So while we live in a world that sometimes looks ugly and feels hopeless, it's important to remember that we do hold the power to affect change. It will require focusing on what we as individuals can control. While the problems may be global, the solutions will be local.

It will be more than reinstituting good manners and extending common courtesy (even though that still goes a long way). It will be about getting back to our humanity and the understanding and the appreciation that we are all interconnected. Each of us, when in the right frame of mind, readily take comfort in our commonality and the bonds we share with one another. Perhaps this has happened to you. You travel somewhere far from where you live or where you grew up. Serendipitously (or not) you meet someone from your town or birthplace. Immediately you celebrate your joint commonality and enjoy some impromptu camaraderie. While you swap stories and recollect familiar places you feel a connection with this complete stranger. So what's going on here? In this situation, you are out of your literal comfort zone and you're clinging to a beacon of familiarity. Any other day when you walk down the streets of your hometown the person you just met would remain a nameless, faceless stranger. But today, as you bond through familiarity, he's a new friend. If you reflect on this, is it fair to recognize that friends are closer than we think? The point here is that how we feel about others and our interactions with them has everything to do with our thinking, which in turn affects our believing. It's all a mirage. It takes discipline to examine objectively the stories we tell ourselves about ourselves and the ones we make up about others. Have the bravery to be objective and honest. And recognize that opinions and generalizations are not facts. The time is now for us to ease our agitated minds and embrace the comfort of our interconnectedness.

In order to create and maintain a civil culture and environment it is important to identify incidents of incivility, such as harassment, and to deal with these incidents quickly and appropriately.

Addressing incidents of incivility as soon as possible is an important preventative measure to reduce the risk of escalating the severity of a behavior and the potential violence. Here are things we can do to practice civility with one another:

1. Focus on others' needs and consider how your words and actions will impact others before you speak or act.

(10 Actions You Can Focus on to Influence Culture of Respect, Civility in your Workplace| Legacy Business Cultures (https://legacycultures.com/)) https://legacycultures.com/10-actions-you-can-focus-on-to-influence-culture-of-respect-civility-in-your-workplace/

Approach each interaction with respect, regardless of whether you believe that the other person's behaviors "earn" or even elicit that respect.

2. Be intentional in your communications.

Plan to listen to the other person without interruption and practice effective listening skills. Develop an awareness of the respect that you display in all areas of your communications, including what you say, how you say it, your voice tone, and the body language that you demonstrate.

3. Appreciate the value of diverse opinions in developing approaches to varying situations.

Recognize that it does not equate to agreement if you listen, clarify what was said, and ask questions to gain an understanding of others' opinions. In situations where disagreement results, learn to "agree to disagree" respectfully.

4. Walk a mile in someone else's shoes.

How easy it is to throw stones, especially when you are convinced of your own righteousness. Never do this, because until you experience exactly what another is experiencing you will never know. Instead of professing moral superiority extend empathy and compassion. A person's situation is their own and how they handle it is intertwined with circumstances and conditions beyond your vantage point. You don't need to know the details to be kind and merciful. And remember there will be a day you will long for the same consideration.

5. Disassociate from Your Negative Emotions.

In the discipline of Mindfulness, there is a concept that you are not your emotions. Instead, you are an objective observer of them. When you put this into practice it can feel empowering. If the emotions of hatred, anger, or frustration come over you, can you muster the discipline to stop and objectively acknowledge what's going on? Yes, these feelings are present within you but you do not have to own them. Recognize the difference between calmly stating "I recognize that I'm feeling agitated" versus exploding with "I am so furious!" Now, I know at first this seems ridiculous. You're in a fury for a reason! We're all human and emotions can often take over in the heat of the moment. But the idea of honing this discipline over time allows for cultivating a baseline of emotional control despite the situational circumstances.

6. Demonstrate Acts of Kindness.

What if we turned our position of guard and retreat into one of expansion and giving through random acts of altruism?

Extending goodwill with no expectation of return pays dividends by elevating your own mood. But also, it has an exponential effect because kindness begets more kindness. It's contagious, as science has proven. When one observes or is subject to this moral elevation it prompts further altruistic behavior towards others. It can become an accelerating upward spiral.

7. Be Optimistic.

This last point is about just deciding to look at the glass as half full. It's a choice. Sometimes a difficult one but it's a commitment to believing that things can and will improve. Life is cyclical and collective animus is hard to sustain much like the energy of a ferocious hurricane. They both will eventually subside. We can each take it upon ourselves to be the contrarian in the group and choose to look on the bright side. Dark clouds eventually dissipate, and sunny days will return.

(Somerville, Christina. 5 things we can do to promote civility in today's society. https://www.convoconnection.com/blog/5-things-we-can-do-to-promote-civility-in-todays-society.)

A synonym of the word civil is humane, as *civility* is an inherent part of our *human condition*. Right now we are exhausted carrying around pent up emotion that needs an overabundance of goodness to balance out. While it feels like a monumental challenge, we can each take steps to just do *our* part. When enough people take this same approach, the civility we all wish for will be ours once again.

The 4C's

My name is Britney Valladares. I'm Guyanese by birth. I was born in the year 2003. I graduated "Best All-Round Student" from Brickdam Secondary in 2019 after writing the CSEC Examinations.

Athletics and Sports are my favorite extracurricular activities. In 2017 and 2018 I competed as a cyclist and in field events (Javelin, Discuss and Shotput) in the country's National Sports Championship Games and walked away with prizes in the Female under 16 &.18and Open races where I gained 2nd and 3rd spaces.

I have always been a very active student; participating in debates is one of my favorite co-curricular activities. As team leader, I led my school through rounds of the JOF Haynes Debating Competition and the Ministry of Health Adolescent Health Debating Competition where we walked away with the winning trophy and prizes and where I was adjudged Best Speaker.

Creating Change for a Better Tomorrow Starts Today

Setting the correct example for my peers is something I aspire to do on a daily basis, though I am not perfect, and I do make my own share of mistakes. I served as Head Prefect for my school between 2018 and 2019. I also sat on our school's Board of Governors as the Student Representative where I was exposed to excellent leadership qualities and decision-making practices. Due to my strong belief in helping others and making a difference in the world, I was honored to be selected for The Leadership Award which is given in honor of strong leadership skills in your life, community, and school for The International Every Girls Wins Award 2021. One person at a time, one day at a time, and one project at a time, I hope to make a difference that will leave a lasting impact on the world.

I'm presently a student attending The Bishops' High School pursuing an Associate Degree in Law. In 2019, I became a Youth Ambassador for The Ministry of Presidency and several other organizations counseling young minds. I additionally partook in the 5th Annual Youth Parliament standing as the Minister of Foreign Affairs where I helped my team to Victory. In 2020, I was elected as the Public Relations Officer for the Girl Build Girl Organization fostering self-confidence, promoting social relationships, building strong interpersonal skills, and reasserting a sense of hope in the future for women.

Aside from academics, I have an extensive background in Electronics and volunteering which has given me significant abilities and skills to aid others around me. I also own and operate three businesses: BV Creative Designs, BV General Constructions, and Winsome Wordsmiths. I write poetry, short stories, and essays and dabble in sketching. In 2019, I gained 2nd Place at the Ministry of Public Health's local Essay Competition on HIV Stigma and

Discrimination. However, I spend most of my free time going on adventures, learning new skills, gaming, or volunteering.

Growing up, I realized that everything I have achieved was due to my inner confidence, self-belief, and where I come from, Guyana. In everything I have accomplished and attained, I never failed to speak it into existence and have myself work towards that goal. Success is not a smooth ride; it comes with potholes, bumps, bottomless pits, etc. We may sometimes fall into any of them, but how we rise from it determines how motivated and robust we are.

Chapter Two

COMMUNITY STARTS THE MOMENT YOU'RE BORN

Betty Speaks

"Embracing community and civility allows us to have genuine hearts while serving, and being served by, others." – Dr. Betty Speaks

Community starts the moment we're born. Our family is the first community we fit into and where we form our personality. How we are treated by our family directly influences our interactions with other people. Many people are completely different inside of their family as opposed to how they act in the outside world. At work, they may come across as introverted and shy, while at home they may be the extroverts who are full of stories. Why is that? It all comes back around to civility and how we treat one another at home and within our community.

As we start to grow up, we build relationships with our neighbors. That's where we may develop different styles of communication or start to form the outside personas we show to strangers. We are taught that we must be "neighborly" to one another, meaning that we are expected to be respectful and polite.

If your family ever entertained pastors or community leaders by asking them over to eat Sunday suppers, then you know exactly what I mean! Back in my day, children were expected to be respectful and to be seen and not heard. Those attitudes have changed some, but children are still expected to respect their elders and to use their best manners whenever they meet someone new.

Our lessons in civility change again once we are old enough to attend school. From the very first moment we step into that Kindergarten classroom, we enter into a large peer group, which is a community made up of other children and adults to whom we must be civil. Teachers, principals, and librarians must be spoken to in a civil tone and we are expected to always "make nice" no matter how badly some other children may have spoken about us to our peers.

Acts of civility are driven by kindness but are also influenced by our perspective. One of the hardest things for us to do is to be completely honest and vulnerable with strangers, or even those who have wronged us, but that is the best way to build strong communities.

P.M. Forni describes the link between community and civility in the following way: "Civility means a great deal more than just being nice to one another. It is complex and encompasses learning how to connect successfully and live well with others, developing thoughtfulness, and fostering effective self-expression and communication. Civility includes courtesy, politeness, mutual respect, fairness, good manners, as well as a matter of good health. Taking an active interest in the well-being of our community and concern for the health of our society is also involved in civility."

As a world ambassador, I frequently find myself in positions of leadership, as a mentor, a speaker, or a guide. In order to be the most helpful, I always check myself before offering any advice or direction so that my thoughts are focused on the other person and not influenced by my personal history.

Now that I am speaking from a global platform, I know that I must become a solutionist, instead of a reactionist. A solutionist is a problem solver, or someone who is fabulous at solving puzzles. As we all know, life is definitely full of puzzles and problems! While it is easier to simply react to life's challenges as they appear, you won't make much of an impact that way.

My life has given me a special set of skills which allow me to motivate, inspire, and help others to improve their lives; one message at a time. It is my hope that by reading these pages you will also become a solutionist and someone who is creating impact in your community.

Before we continue, I think it's important that I tell you a little bit about myself. My life has had its ups and downs, just like so many others. My younger years were tough and I had a difficult childhood. As a baby, I was raised by my loving grandparents up until the time I was around five years old. One day, my birth mother, a woman whom I had never even met, re-entered my life and said that she wanted to take me back with her and join her other family hundreds of miles away.

The day we met is the same day she took me away from the home and community where I had been raised. In the new community my mother took me to, I was rarely treated with civility. When my mother took me back to her home and introduced me to my stepfather and my half siblings, I had to learn the rules of the new community I had entered. I received spankings because I didn't call my mother "mom" and my stepfather "dad," and the neighborhood kids would tease me and call me a bastard child.

Later in life, I joined the Army and faced additional adversity as an African American female. I have been a part of so many communities through the years and in that time, I have learned the value of staying true to yourself no matter what your peers may say.

Following your true, spiritual, path can sometimes be very lonesome. That's why, whenever I am speaking to someone who feels like an outsider, I feel an intense amount of empathy for that person; I have stood in their shoes many times.

One of our American founding fathers, Benjamin Franklin, once said, "Be civil to all; serviceable to many; familiar with few; friend to one; enemy to none."

I try to live by that same sentiment and do my best to maintain my civility when encountering people outside of my community or those with different points of view. Even though those words are not written anywhere in our Declaration of Independence or in the

U.S. Constitution, I think that they really do sum up the value systems we hold dear.

Today, while I am writing these pages, my thoughts turn to the acts committed against those same values on January 6th, 2021, when rioters stormed the United States Capitol. As an Army veteran, I have fought and nearly died to defend the country symbolized by the United States' red, white, and blue flag. When I saw that same flag taken down and replaced by flags bearing someone's name, or symbols of oppression, I was hurt.

We know that children are the future. As their elders, we must ignite in them the desire to build communities built upon civility and morality. God granted us each the gift of discernment, which is the process of determining God's desire in a situation or for one's life or identifying the true nature of a thing, such as discerning whether a thing is good or evil, right or wrong.

There was no civility in the crowd of rioters that day and I can't help but think that their gifts of discernment were silenced by their anger. I believe that such a terrible thing would never have happened if the protests that day had remained civil.

The political commentator, Van Jones, sums up the importance of civil discussion in our society as, "Civility isn't just some optional value in a multicultural, multistate democratic republic. Civility is the key to civilization."

Let's take a closer look at that word, "civil." Just like P.M Forni described earlier, to be civil means that you are both courteous and polite.

That being said, kindness and civility are closely related and can sometimes be confused. Here's an example of that difference from my own life. When I was deployed as a soldier to Saudi Arabia back in the 1990's, I learned that when civility is misconstrued as kindness it can result in profoundly mixed signals. As a member of the armed forces, I was trained to protect and defend my fellow soldiers, my countrymen and women, and the innocent townspeople where we were stationed.

One day, I encountered an Arabian man and treated him in what I thought was a civil manner. Unbeknownst to me at the time, my brand of American, civil, politeness was perceived by the man as extremely kind or even flirty behavior. After only a few interactions, the man was convinced that he must make me one of his wives.

He came to see me every day and then he started to bring me gifts. We were told in training to never accept gifts from the locals as they might be concealing bombs so I would politely decline every time. As a Christian, I trust my gut and my gift of discernment.

Whenever I would look the man in the eyes, I saw no evil there. Just captivating brown irises and a sincere expression. I tried telling him that I was married, but it didn't do any good.

I remember that he came to make sure I was safe after the bombing at our base on June 26th, 1996. Twenty-three of my fellow soldiers were killed that day and more than 300 people wounded. My admirer was so relieved that I was safe, he tried to bring me a cake.

I haven't thought about that man in years, and the memory of our interactions makes me wonder. Was I kind to him? Was he civil to me? Should I have been less civil and made him go away sooner?

Today, I understand that the man was harassing me and that by remaining civil, I made it harder for both of us in the aftermath of the bombings. Even though I thought that I was being civil, the man perceived my actions as my desire for him to continue his romantic pursuit of my heart.

Looking back, I know why I was hesitant to speak up before I did; because the situation made me feel so vulnerable. I was afraid to take the risk of making the man angry and turning one of his love gifts into a weapon.

The tragedy on June 26th made me understand that the harassment had to come to an end. I was a superior officer, not to mention a mentor, to many young women and men in our troop and it was my duty to set an example. That day, I told my story to my commanding officers and they, along with the local police, intervened and told the man to stay away

The moment I decided to take action and report the man's actions, I felt in my soul that I was making the right choice. My thoughts turned to my second grandmother, Mable, her voice, and her community. Whenever I was in the well of sorrow, anxiety, or fear, I would hear her voice in my head singing the gospel hymn "Walk with Me, Lord."

Every time her voice reached me, I would have an epiphany that would guide my steps and help me make the right decision. When I was a kid and my mother took me away from my biological grandparents, I found a second grandmother in that town where I was forced to live. My newly found grandmother showed me the importance of community and faith. It's so interesting to think about now, but back when I was a kid people used to tell me that I looked just like my grandmother. We didn't share even a single drop of blood, but people thought we looked alike because there was a lot of love between us and we were always together. Her affection was worth more to me back then than anything.

My grandma Mable's voice, and her song, still live inside my heart. I am as old today as she was back when she took me under her wing and walked me to church, protecting me from the gossip and the stares of parishioners who preferred to judge than to understand. She helped teach me a very important lesson.

Christians who gossip about other Christians are not truly Christian. Instead of talking about one another, we should pray for one another. We may never know what sort of things our fellow church goers or community members are going through.

When I was twelve years old, I was baptized and I gave my life to Christ. When I waded into the water of that cool natural spring hole, I felt the light of the Lord touch my heart. That day, I entered a community that has given my life true meaning: the community of the Christian faith. I felt connected to other people who carried the word of the Lord in their hearts, whose faithful songs lifted my spirit above the petty gossip and whispers so that I could find my way on to the path which has led me to this very moment.

In the Bible, Hebrews 10:24-25 says, "And let us consider how we may spur one another on toward love and good deeds, not giving up meeting together, as some are in the habit of doing, but encouraging one another—and all the more as you see the Day approaching."

God made us in HIS image and wants us to be like HIM. Jesus asked that all of our sins be carried with him when he went to the cross. So, when we go about building our communities, we must remember to be courageous enough to stand up and remind others that we must stand up for what is right and to live righteously in civility. We must build our communities on the pillars of civility and morality.

The great Martin Luther King, Jr. describes our relationship to one another as, "Whatever affects one directly affects all indirectly." That quote is so powerful, and so true.

On this tedious journey of life, we need to show our children unconditional love so that they can show that same unconditional love to others. Kids don't know what they are being born into, what the world is really like. Life isn't always kind and the journey we must take on this earth is tedious compared to the peace we will one day find in the Kingdom of God.

That is why we must raise our children in communities of faith and love which start inside of our families. Whenever I am unsure of what to do next, I read the word of God and think about the day when I gave my life to Christ and put all of my life's worry and sin upon that cross.

My grandmother, Mable, taught me that we must never stop walking in HIS image. Now, as an adult, I can see and respect how she helped mend the broken pieces of the child I was back then with the best possible material...the word of God. She taught me old fashioned religion and how to be civil.

Civility really is a beautiful word and I think it's a very feminine word. To me, it's a word similar to something like beauty. We, as women, live our lives according to the ideals of civil behavior. As young girls, we are taught that to be a lady, one must act according to the rules of civilized society. We have a natural desire to take care of people, to raise children, and to make safe homes. We carry civility in our hearts and then into our communities.

Jean Vanier once said, "One of the marvelous things about community is that it enables us to welcome and help people in a way we couldn't as individuals. When we pool our strength and share the work and responsibility, we can welcome many people, even those in deep distress, and perhaps help them find self-confidence and inner healing."

Our communities start at home and then spread into our neighborhood, our schools, our churches, and even onto our social media circles. You know in your heart what is right and your story, your input, is an invaluable thread in the tapestry that is your community. Shake off your fear, cast your doubts aside, and strengthen your heart with the grace of the Holy Spirit so that your light may help guide the way of those in your community who are lost in the dark.

The 4C's

One of my very favorite words that relates to our role in our communities is something you won't find in any dictionary, at least not yet! That word is "ACTIONCUTION." It's a combination of action and execution. To ensure that our communities are safe, we must take "ACTIONCUTION" and treat one another in a civil manner.

Believe it or not, some State officials are even referred to as civility ambassadors! The National Foundation for Women Legislators describes something called the "Pillars of Civility." Some of those pillar's state that, "Participating in democracy requires knowing each other. Outside forces are constantly introducing incivility to your legislature. Constituents — both friendly and opposing — are more and more polarized in their thinking and media outlets quickly amplify events and actions."

You see, some people simply don't understand how to be civil because they were raised in a community without love or because they weren't taught those life lessons as a child. With the prevalence of social media in our society, people who are ignorant or malicious have the exact same platform as the rest of us and it is up to the righteous among us to spread messages of love and equity in a civil manner.

So, if you encounter someone in your community who isn't acting civil, or someone is trying to enter your community with a less than civil attitude, what are you going to do? I suggest that you take things back to the basics. Treat people with love and be kind. Choose civility and become an ambassador in your community to the world.

Carry this quote with you on your journey as a civility ambassador, "Never doubt that a small group of thoughtful, committed citizens can change the world; indeed, it's the only thing that ever has." - Margaret Mead

I ask you today to share your light and your gifts with the world so that we may create a more civil global community.

Yours in love and in spirit, Dr. Betty Speaks

Dr. BETTY SPEAKS is retired with HONORS from the United States Army, an award winning I Change Nations International Speaker, Global Network Virtual Marketer and Entrepreneur, 8x Best Selling Collaborate Author, Jesus Woman at Godheads Ministry, Ambassador to the Pink Pul-Pit International Ministry, Intentional Master Story Teller, Certified Black Belt Speaker plus she has been featured on TV shows and a host of Radio broadcasting. When Betty Speaks… she Speaks!

Dr. BETTY SPEAKS is that power voice for those silenced by traumatic situations throughout their journey in LIFE. Her mission is to help others who have remanences of their experiences to destroy the silence and SOAR. Her transparent story of grief, depression, and healing, along with her strategies for the inspiration to SOAR, will help them to know they can do the same. As a World Ambassador and a genuine leader to all she encountered, she realized that she needed to be the first to speak out so she can effectively inspire others to SOAR. A global leader, a global executive coach, and an international author; She has devoted her influential voice to Podcasting a phenomenal global show "Overcoming Battles by Being Strong and Courageous" A Life Change Now! Plus, featured on the Power of Praise Network! Inspiring others to SOAR with H.O.P.E:

S.O.A.R Seize Opportunities and Rise

H.O.P.E Help Other People Enjoy Life

Dr. Speaks is your Life Servant Leader! She is extremely passionate with empowering individuals to establish themselves through the four components of LIFE (Spiritual Growth, Financial Literacy, Personal and Professional Development). She's that chosen warrior who declares victory as opposed to being vindictive.

Readers can connect with Dr. BETTY SPEAKS at:
www.bettyspeaks.com;

Facebook: https://www.facebook.com/betty.speaks.92;

Instagram: https://www.instagram.com/bettyspeaks

The 4C's

Chapter Three

CIVILIST ON THE RISE

Beauty Razack

Civility means a great deal more than just being nice to one another. It is complex and encompasses learning how to connect successfully and live well with others, developing thoughtfulness, and fostering effective self-expression and communication. Civility includes courtesy, politeness, mutual respect, fairness, good manners, as well as a matter of good health. Taking an active interest in the well-being of our community and concern for the health of our society is also involved in civility." – P.M. Forni

I am 17 years old and a Civilist on the rise. Civilist is probably a word that you're not that familiar with; it's not in common parlance. It means a person who makes efforts to live by a moral code, someone who is determined to be a decent citizen. The word "civility" is derived from that, and the original definition of civility is citizens prepared towards giving of themselves for the betterment of the commonwealth and for the greater good for all involved. I'm hoping that in this piece of literature we'll find a few new ways to be civil and hopefully, it will be in accordance with the original definition of civility.

The 4C's

A great problem of mine is that civility has become a dirty word in many countries. And in part, that's because modern usage equates civility with formal politeness, formal behavior and we've gotten away from the idea of citizenship.

Our virtual world seems to have been stolen by persons who hide behind nicknames and initials to unleash vitriol, and hate and – what probably upsets me just as much – people who are more than ready to tell you what they think and yet not so quick to confess who they are. When did it become okay to savage someone along with their opinion? The explosion of reality television shows that offer us a chance to witness public embarrassment and pile abuse on those we despise.

Things are not that better when you look at what is happening in the world as it relates to politics. Simply having a different political opinion seems to be reason enough for some to demonize those on the other side of the political spectrum. Providing a country with wise and compassionate leadership seems to take a back seat to demonstrating how intellectually superior one party's position is vs the others. Reports of stormed parliaments and brawling MPs scarcely seem to raise eyebrows in our morally anaesthetized times. While some of our leaders have probably earned at least a part of the opprobrium heaped upon them on the airwaves and over the internet, we need to remember that criticizing an institution sets up a dangerous precedent; by the time "our" man or woman is in charge, the basis upon which we would expect others to respect their position will have been eroded or irreparably damaged.

And with all that has been happening, what in the world are we teaching our children, our youth, the future of our countries and the world at large? As experts in civility would have noted, it is challenging for the society we now live in to expect or demand that teenagers and children stop bullying and tormenting each other, given the example aforementioned they would have developed the behavior of the adults and political leaders surrounding them. Let's put some steadiness back into our discourse.

It would definitely be the attitude of arrogance and even blindness to assume that everyone feels the same way and commentaries are requested so that others can share their perspectives from their equally restricted views.

In my opinion, people are entitled to their opinions without being sneered at, insulted or derided. The fact that we are rife with the technological advancements that enables us to communicate with thousands of people certainly shouldn't require us to say, post and do things online that we wouldn't say when physically facing someone. Hiding behind the keyboard doesn't advance our goals or our society and we shouldn't try to utilize it as a tool to do so.

If it is that the measure of our society is equal in proportion to the measure of our civility, we then have to wonder whether technology is really serving us well or in the appropriate manner, so to speak. "Civility is not a sign of weakness," as the late US President John F. Kennedy once said. Civility means treating others respectfully, regardless of what we think of them or what we feel they deserve. It is definitely time to check ourselves and put our traditional values back into our discourse. It is time for each and every one of us to take the personal responsibility for what we say and how we say it and return our societies to a state of reason.

Let's take into consideration the crowd that swarmed the Capitol on January 6th was ill-prepared to mount an insurrection and seize power, performing a coup de grâce to civility but coming well shy of delivering a revolutionary punch.

A few of its sections are surely "counting coup" in expectation of another act, to lift a scoring description from Native American warrior-lore.

The late Paul Krassner would have likely named this action a staggering formation, the activists relaxing their muscles amid stiffening grandiloquence and a petering police presence. And it's the Youth International Party, the society he co-founded in the late 1960s to protest the acquisitiveness and fierceness, especially with respect to the Vietnam War, of American life, that claims to offer a useful frame of orientation to comprehend this breakout.

Being born in Guyana, but also witnessing the many cases of injustices in not just my country but the Caribbean and the diaspora, has taught me resilience and that there must be strength over silence if we're to promote civility. We were taught by the actions of our leaders that justice can only come if we're on top of a certain aspect of the social structure, that finance is the key to all opportunities, and that, regardless of how qualified you are, what is important is the close contact you have to those in the positions you're hoping to be connected with.

Violence and Abuse are just two of the many expressions of incivility worldwide; allow me to place emphasis on the recent gruesome killings of so many women in the Caribbean. The world we live in has its flaws when it comes to the safety and security of its most valuable assets; it's human resources and the actions taken by our political leaders are quite limited. There is a great need for us to all come together, to take a stand and raise awareness, to ensure that justice is served and we promote peace.

Another great area of error on our part, not just in Guyana but globally, is Racism; the division by ethnicity has hindered our growth as a nation politically, socially and economically.

However, in Guyana it is clear that we do not see political parties as being representatives of the entire country but as representatives of a particular ethnic group.

Even though we know that Racism is not a new phenomenon, in today's modern world, which claims to be enlightened in so many ways, it can come as a surprise that it still thrives with great prevalence. While there are many persons who promote diversity and appreciate the variances between those of different religions and cultures, there are also many others who see those races and religions as a threat and the result of this intolerance in our society does have its far reaching consequences. But the big questions are where has it stemmed from and have we realized the economic effects it has on global developments?

What happens if Racism continues to Thrive?

It's no lie that a country with a racist mentality does not give all of its citizens the opportunity to contribute collectively to the nation, thus this is a limiting factor for its successes and development.

This racist mentality breeds an environment in which an entire class of people cannot benefit from the same privileges as the rest of society, and lack the educational and employment opportunities that would permit them to contribute to the overall economic well-being of their country through essential sectors such as medicine, economics or technology. Also, by limiting one race's ability to partake and contribute fully in the culture of the country, the people as a whole are incapable of appreciating and understanding the resemblances and variances between them, resulting in social inaction and continuing determination of racism through upcoming generations. On a more basic level, if racism is permitted to thrive within society as a whole, there is no doubt that eventually this will lead to aggression and even violence on a local or even national scale. If the bad feeling is allowed to form between community groups, over time this unquestionably will result in first low level negativity, from the small act of name calling and isolated incidents to potentially full scale conflict. Warfare and rioting can be the result of this racist predisposition and intolerance.

Now, allow me to highlight the American Civil Rights Movement of the late 1950s/60s and the major contributing factors of this occurrence in the history of the struggle for freedom.

In an article published by the Nations Magazine, it was stated 'The mass protest movement against racial segregation and discrimination in the southern US came to national prominence during the mid-1950s. This undertaking had its backgrounds in the centuries-long efforts of enslaved Africans and their descendants to resist racial oppression and to abolish the institution of slavery'.

Though enslaved people were liberated as a result of the Civil War and were then approved to have basic civil rights through the passage of the Fourteenth and Fifteenth amendments to the US Constitution, the fight continued to secure federal protection of these rights during the next century. "Through nonviolent protest, the civil rights movement of the 1950s and '60s hoped to break the pattern of public facilities' being segregated by race in

the South and attained the greatest and key development in the equal-rights law making for African Americans ever since the Rebuilding period of (1865–77). Although the passage in 1964 and 1965 of major civil rights legislation was victorious for the movement, by then militant Black activists had begun to see their fight as a self-determination or freedom movement not just seeking civil rights improvements but instead challenging the continuing economic, political, and cultural penalties of past racial oppression". (Carson, Clayborn. American civil rights movement. www.brittanica.com/event/American-civil-rights-movment).

American history has been manifested by the tireless efforts to expand the scope and inclusiveness of civil rights. Even though equal rights for all were confirmed in the founding documents of the United States, many of the new country's occupants were deprived of their basic rights.

However, regardless of these laws, black Americans did not, in any way, attain economic equality. Although there has been significant progress since the Civil Rights Movement, black Americans still remain a socially disadvantaged group and this is also another relating factor for blacks generally.

If I'm to now highlight the works of Dr. Maya Angelou, in her tribute to the fiftieth anniversary of the United Nations, "A Brave and Startling Truth," said that "We must confess that we are the possible…. We are the miraculous, the true wonders of this world." And Angelou was one of the wonders of the world. We need to understand that we are the change we want to see if only we would do what is acceptable and what is Just.
https://www.thenation.com/archive/artice/Maya -Angelou's- Civil - Rights- Legacy.

Maya Angelou was also not only a participant in the civil rights struggles of the 1950s and 1960s but "Maya Angelou showed the injustice in society and gave an in-depth view of how blacks were treated. There is no lie that Civil Rights has a major influence in our world in numerous ways. People should not be judged for their skin color, but by who they are." Angelou worked as an outspoken Civil Rights activist during the movement. But even after the Civil Rights Movement had ended, Angelou continued to be a voice of humanity, being an agent of change and standing up against anything that harmed the human spirit in any way. Angelou progressed to influence the American society as a whole, from the 1970s to the day she died, May 28, 2014. She was a multi-talented person as Toni Morrison, a friend and contemporary of Angelou, expressed: "She had 19 talents and used 10. And she was a real original."

After listing a variety of situations that are uncivil, how can we now be the solution? What is the importance of creativity? How can we utilize creativity as our best problem-solving tool for all issues including this one?

Breaking past conventional barriers. Creativity is important for breaking through conventional barriers to advancement. Just for instance, if you run into a complex problem that's always been solved a certain way, with a handful of disadvantages, you may be able to eliminate those disadvantages with a creative new approach.

Finding optimal solutions. Coming up with your own ideas is also a way to get closer to "optimal" solutions. If you were to generate just a few ideas, you'd have limited options for how to move onward. Through creativity, you can generate a few more, and you'll have a much better chance at improving upon your "first instinct" approaches giving rise to promoting civility, but what other actions should be taken?

We first need to organize efforts to have civility rebirthed.

Regardless of this disconsolate picture, it's encouraging to know there are small glimmers of hope out there. There are groups, organizations and foundations developing that are rife with leaders who are pleading and working towards a return to common courtesy, civility, and respectful exchange.

"Civility does not ... mean the mere outward gentleness of speech cultivated for the occasion, but an inborn gentleness and desire to do the opponent good." - Mahatma Gandhi

It may often seem the mere utterance of Please Be Kind is barely a whisper compared to the incessant screaming of cruel debate.

Some media organizations are deciding to focus on the positive and to reaffirm how we are all connected and how important this all is, thus its worthy to be celebrated.

Reflecting on Our Own Efforts to Extend Civility.

While we live in a world that sometimes appears to be ugly and often feels hopeless, it's crucial to remember that we do hold the power to be the change and all it requires is focusing on what we as citizens can control. While the problems may be global, the solutions will be local; however, we at BlessedGirls International are hoping that this is changed so that our solutions have a more global impact.

It will definitely take more than reinstituting good manners and extending common courtesy, even though that still goes a long way. It will be focused on regaining our humanity and the understanding that we are all connected in some way or the other. Each of us, when we are in the right and just frame of mind, readily take ease in our unity and the bonds we share with one another.

Another crucial element up for discussion in this chapter and as a part of the 4Cs movement is another global crisis, one that is equally as important as civility, that being Climate Change.

But what really is climate change? Climate change could be referred to as a change in global or regional climate patterns. Climate change may also be the causal factor making weather patterns less predictable.

Sadly, us human beings are great contributors to this phenomenon; throughout most of human history, and certainly, before human beings emerged as a dominant species throughout the world, all climate changes were the direct result of natural forces, such as the solar cycles and volcanic eruptions. Due to the Industrial Revolution and the increase in the size of the population, however, us humans began altering climates with ever-growing effect, and eventually exceeded the natural causes in their capacity to change the climate. The Human-caused global climate change is predominantly due to the discharge, through our activities, of greenhouse gases.

The greenhouse gases are released into the air, where they stay for a very long period of time at high altitude hence, they absorb heat by reflecting sunlight. This then causes the atmosphere, the surface of the land, and the oceans to become warm. There is no doubt that various aspects of our activities contribute greatly to the greenhouse gases in the atmosphere.

Yes, if you were to argue with me, Fossil Fuels carry much of the responsibility. The process of burning fossil fuels produces a variety of pollutants, as well as a significant greenhouse gas, carbon dioxide. We know that the use of gasoline and diesel to power vehicles is a large contributor, but, overall, transportation only accounts for approximately 14% of total greenhouse gas emissions.

The single largest culprit is electricity production by coal, gas, or oil-burning power plants, causing 20% of all emissions.

But there's a twist to this situation, we are the cause, and we are also the solution! Knowing that our actions are the main drivers of global warming helps us to understand how and why our climate is changing, and it noticeably defines the issue as one that is within our power to address.

It's obvious that we cannot avoid some level of the warming caused by the heat-trapping gases already present in the atmosphere. It's important to note that some of the gases (such as carbon dioxide and nitrous oxide) will last for more than a century to come. But with aggressive measures to reduce future emissions and adapt to those climate impacts we cannot avoid; we have a small window to avoid the worst climate change harms and to re- build a better and safer world.

What does all of that mean? It means that we should be investing in a clean energy economy, one that is healthier and more livable and resilient to communities. It means converting

transportation, reorienting our food system, and shifting to lower-carbon lifestyles. It means fighting the deception spread by fossil fuel companies and other wealthy interests. It also means fighting for equity and environmental fairness for all.

A question you may be asking yourself, "How can we implement education for climate action and climate justice?"

Years of climate activism and advocacy at the policy level are on the cusp of bearing fruit in 2021. And youth climate activists like myself around the world will continue to bring new voices, including feminist climate leadership, and new entry points, like girls' education and climate justice, into climate decision making and solutions.

As discussions about climate change and education begin to shift from policy advocacy to policy implementation, stakeholders and leaders will be looking for resources and frameworks to diagnose, strategize, and propose for the urgent reorientation of their education systems to carbon neutrality and climate literacy. While addressing the carbon footprint of education infrastructure is also an important factor (e.g. the energy efficiency of school buildings or food waste), the most difficult task at hand is to ensure that teaching and learning across all curricular areas of kindergarten - high school, higher education, and career and technical education are oriented not just toward achieving climate literacy, but also toward climate action and climate justice.

This task goes beyond the reformation of the curricular, which is aimed at adding climate change and environmental notions into the already existing curriculum. While a critical step, such reformative change permits the education sector to continuously avoid confronting its fundamental problem of purpose — that is, the purpose of a 21st century education system that is designed for the days of the Developed Revolution.

Constrained by the urgency of runaway climate change and environmental collapse, the task of shifting from advocating for education for climate action to developing education for climate action will require policymakers to identify trails to the deeper ontological change of education.

This destination – a new green learning agenda – purposes to serve as a turning compass toward a more essential vision of education. At its core, this new green learning agenda seeks to redress social inequalities intensified by the climate crisis (and the COVID-19 pandemic) first by cultivating and understanding the awareness that the health of human society is interwoven with the health of the planet. And secondly, it pursues to redress injustices by developing the extensiveness of green skills across a person's lifetime that is essential to increase humanity's shared resilience and adaptive capacity. Achieving these twin objectives means simultaneously addressing gender and racial inequality and a learning catastrophe that is redefined as the incapability of our education systems to teach children, youth, and adults how to live within planetary boundaries.

If I am to highlight at least one climate activist who has made valuable contributions towards this phenomenon, it would definitely be Greta Thunberg. There is so much that we can all learn from her sense of bravery when standing up in front of the global community targeting such an important issue in our world.

When Greta Thunberg began her speech to the United Nations, it was very clear from the inception that her speech to the world leaders would be diverse.

"My message is that we'll be watching you."

The line was packaged by applause and some laughs, but her expression signaled that this was no amusing matter to her. If you listen to the scientists, as Thunberg advised congress to do a few months ago, it's quite easy to understand why. Angry Thunberg tells the world leaders she 'will never forgive' them for failing on properly addressing climate change. If our planet remains warming, the results will definitely be frightening. This 16-year-old's fiery speech was a revolutionary movement that has been given new determination by a group of savvy young leaders.

The 4C's

All over the world, young people are progressively leading the push to address climate change. They are filing lawsuits, marching in the streets in massive numbers, and compelling world leaders to act and to act fast.

But based on the pale commitments to reduce planet-warming emissions that were announced at the UN Climate Summit and the absence of major polluters from the stage entirely, the key world leaders still aren't willing to take the transformative action scientists say we need to be able to get rid of the global economy and its fossil fuel dependence.

The science is clearer than ever; we need to act now. And to do so, the adults in power will have to listen to the kids of today; which is why I decided to include this issue in my chapter.

"Rapid, far-reaching and unprecedented changes in all aspects of society."

This was the message from a dire report from the Intergovernmental Panel on Climate Change (IPCC) that detailed what needs to be done to keep global warming below 1.5 degrees Celsius above pre-industrial levels.

But that account was delivered nearly a year ago. Since then, more alarming evidence of the damage humans are doing on the planet has arisen. The concentration of carbon dioxide in the atmosphere continues to rise, and Earth endured its hottest month in July 2016.

Despite the perseverance conveyed by scientists and expressed by the growing youth movement, some world leaders don't appear to be heeding their calls.

It is important to remember that the conditions of the climate in a region which was considered to be that region's specialty are also changing. The plants and animals that would have survived in a particular climate are now facing difficulties in their areas of survival.

We all know that the main cause of the change of climate is global warming which is causing the weather situations of a climate that is different and difficult for the current species.

We need to take into consideration that climate change does not happen over a few days; it takes a lot of time. Do not underestimate the power of the people. We've seen an almost overnight change in behavior in relation to plastics. We're currently seeing something similar, if slower, in people's attitudes towards water, with more and more of us taking care and using it wisely. It has become publicly intolerable to litter or to use throwaway plastic bags. It is increasingly socially unacceptable to waste water. The same thing can happen – and maybe is happening – with regard to behavior which stokes climate change.

One last chunk of positive news: while it may cost a lot of money to respond successfully to climate change, we can afford it. Research has shown that is the best possible investment we could possibly make. It would be much costlier if we do not respond. And the economic benefits of moderating and familiarizing to climate change in terms of damage contained, extra growth achieved through new investment and infrastructure, and prosperity boosted through innovative technology.

Remember, the scandal is not that climate change is made up. The scandal is that it's not, and that while a lot has already been done to tackle it, we are still not doing as well as we could. Maybe a question we should all ask ourselves is: Why is it that tackling climate is not at the top of everyone's agenda? There's no doubt, because most people have eventful lives and other things to worry about. Partly because the effects of a changing climate tend to be unseen and incremental until they are suddenly catastrophic. And maybe, too, because of the words we often use. Language is such a crucial element, so here's my final thought: if words like "climate change" and "global warming" have become a turn off for most ordinary people, maybe we should switch the words we use.

Perhaps if we were to talk instead about what those things literally mean: killer weather, a world under water, and a pledged future.

Many people might not find it necessary to fight against something that sounds elusively technical and non-threatening like climate change. But pretty much all of us would do so to protect our loved ones, our livelihoods and to build a better world. Climate change is too real to be good. So let's tell it like it is, let's walk the walk and not just talk that talk, let's tackle it together, and let's redouble our efforts. Over the past 200+ years humans have comprehensively established that they can change the climate and we have changed it for the worse because we are constantly doing the wrong things. Now let's show we can change it for the better by doing all of the right things together.

Creating Change for a Better Tomorrow Starts Today

I introduce to you, Beauty Roshani Razack. She was born on the 4th October in the year 2003, and is now seventeen (17) years of age. Beauty Razack is from the only English speaking country located in South America (Guyana) and is of Guyanese Descent.

Miss Razack attended the St. Cuthbert's Nursery and Primary Schools respectively, and upon writing the National Grade Six Assessment was offered a Scholarship by the Ministry of Amerindian Affairs, thus giving her the opportunity to attend Secondary School in the Capital City (Georgetown). She has recently completed her secondary education at the Richard Ishmael Secondary School where she attended for the five-year period, and where she also managed to secure passes in twenty-one (21) subjects at the 2020 Caribbean Secondary Examination Council (CSEC).

Beauty Razack would have recently represented Guyana at the Caribbean Youth Ambassadors Program held in the United States last August, aimed at promoting leadership and civility among the countries in the Western hemisphere. However, her sense of participation and ambassadorial positions are not just limited to that specific program. She is a Change-maker with UNITE2030 (an initiative that falls under the works of the United Nations). The Global Peace Chain also appointed her as one of the Global Peace Ambassadors for the years (2020-2022). This beauty is the country representative for the Global Youth Model United Nation (GYMUN), Country Director and Representative at the International Crisis Summit (ICS), Representative at UNFPA Caribbean, Advocate at UN Women Caribbean, Ambassador at Blessed Girls Global Chapter, Representative at the International Affairs Committee (IAC), Deputy country Coordinator at the International Youth Summit (IYS), United Nations Sustainable Development Goals (SDG) Ambassador, Member of Cure Violence and Foundation for Environmental Education among other local and International bodies that deal with the affairs of youth and the social ills of our global community.

Just a few months ago, the Talk African Foundation nominated her as one of the most beautiful and influential women of the world.

Each of these positions is a dominant effect on her passion for volunteerism and on being an instrument of change as she aids in serving her community and country at large.

Beauty Razack has recently started the University of Guyana and the University of Peking doing a Degree in Petroleum Engineering and Law as she has the hope of pursuing both law and engineering. She firmly believes that a person or individual should not be limited to just one career path.

Creating Change for a Better Tomorrow Starts Today

For further information, Miss Razack can be contacted on the following:

Contact Number: (592) 644-6954

Email: roshanirazack141@gmail.com

Regards,

Beauty Roshani Razack

The 4C's

Chapter Four

CIVILITY BEGINS WITH ONE INDIVIDUAL

Tamia Louissant

We are striving to forge a union with purpose/To compose a country committed to all cultures, colors, characters and conditions of man/ And so we lift our gazes not to what stands between us but what stands before us/ We close the divide because we know, to put our future first, we must first put our differences aside" (Gorman, Amanda. The hill we climb. Lines 34-35).

The definition of civility's depths runs deeper than the overall interpretation of representing and showing great virtues and etiquette. In "The Hill We Climb," Amanda Gorman talks about putting our differences aside; this represents the sense of togetherness that civility brings. Essentially, she calls for civility within everyone, that we should announce the great things that are before us and not focus strongly on the wrongdoings in the world. She calls on us to reconcile with any hardships or trials and she wrote about this in a respectful manner without attacking anyone's incivility.

Acknowledging harm and moving towards resolutions with accountability is a main root in civility. Civility begins with one individual and has a butterfly effect on everyone else. What should be acknowledged is that there is no limit to who can show civility. No rules come to play in "who should be civil, at what age can I be civil, when can I start being civil?". Hence, as I write on this excellent topic of civility, I would like to emphasize that it does not matter the age, sex, or ethnicity someone is as they pursue civility. Everyone on this planet has come across a variety of struggles, whether it's mental, financial, physical, or emotional, we all have endured the feelings of pain. If we endure all different kinds of pain, a main interest should be finding happiness and civility is a start to that. One of the best things about civility is that it relates to every last human being.

There is not only one standard civility is involved with, but there are also a variety of elements that make up civility. Some of those elements might be leadership, social intelligence, influence, service and much more. It is crucial to express what civility is and what it is about because it can make or break anything. Our country, our life, our family, and in a way even ourselves. Civility is also important because it brings a sense of calming behavior into existence. It is becoming rare to find someone who can express civility, but once civility is found, so is peace. Being civil is a task that comes within the purest form of our hearts and should be genuinely expressed.

Civility should be shown at all times because there is no logical reason to be uncivil. Throughout every aspect of our life we should be expressing civility to affect another's life and ultimately the world. Civility should not be forced upon others and should come in a natural manner so, therefore, we are not picking and choosing when civility should be shown. Civility comes from our hearts, through love, and is mainly learned over time with experience.

Civility is also found within the decency of having patience on a daily basis. It takes a lot of your character to express civility because of the tempting tool that entices us to act outside of civil behavior. When having patience we find civility, as well, because when communicating there are no closed minds, which is crucial when having a key conversation.

In my view, civility means having the decency to perform kind acts, no matter the circumstance. To be there for your peers, neighbors, family members, bosses and, most importantly, strangers in the best way possible. Above all else, civility should be executed in a dignified manner. This all applies even when facing challenges and stepping out of your comfort zone results in an issue; responding with civility means acting in a way that delivers a message in a respectful manner. Civility means nothing if you don't show genuine care and respect towards others, their opinions, or even their concerns. Having civility means to have manners, courtesy and most importantly, honor. Respect goes a long way, it should not be overlooked because the impact it has on others is major. Going above and beyond to show those random acts of kindness, being open and honest to any situation, or even simply just reaching out. Those small actions of courtesy that we make, and should make, gives civility more clarity. The clarity of the fact we are all here for each other, to live out all expectations and make someone feel true support.

It is significant to realize the theme of togetherness that the intention of being civil brings. The understanding of being civil comes from being considerate and not hesitant to make sure others are treated in a dignified way. Not only is being civil beneficial to the individuals being impacted, but also to your own personal wellbeing. Civility adds to my life drastically in ways seen and unseen. As a sixteen

The 4C's

year old African American woman, civility is something that I have developed from my household. It starts as simple as having manners; from saying please and thank you, to showing appreciation towards others and what they have done for me. With that experience I have adapted civility into my own life, which has made me the humble, gracious young lady I am today. I've developed the mindset over time to be friendly towards others all the time no matter what because, regardless of outward appearances, you don't know what that person is going through. Without me realizing, this was one of the ways I would express my civility.

Civility adds to my life in ways unseen because my kindhearted actions rub off on others. Others are able to see my authentic self and always recall who I am based on one productive conversation with me. There are always people watching, whether we know it or not; this knowledge should inspire me, and should inspire more people, to try to want to be the reason someone smiles. My passion for having civility in my life is bold because I've developed my character and personal integrity in a dignified manner. Personally, I love doing all that I can to see others happy and see a smile on their faces. It is just one of my personal habits to check up on my friends to make sure they are good, and sometimes I tend to put them before myself.

My passion for civility is also strong because of my eagerness to be successful. I believe that giving your all into others will pour back into you and to being successful – that is one of the keys. In order for me to stay positive about getting all that I can acquire in life then being humble is a resource that is necessary.

Civility has a major impact on my life daily. Since civility is about respect, it constantly is brought up in my life; how I talk to others, help them, and always make sure to be my best positive self no matter who the person is. It's important to be civil towards others because it builds an amazing character for yourself. I believe that always having true intentions towards others has built my personality even stronger and continues to daily.

Just me showing civility and others showing civility adds to our lives by enhancing our minds with the perspectives of others. It brings them to conclusions that there are positive people out in the world that care and have respect for them, and even their thoughts/ideas. Civility has helped me overcome lots of challenges especially in my high school experience. As a young woman attending an all girls' school has its pros and cons like everything in life. Something I managed to overcome by having the tool of civility was being able to confront others. When people hear the word confront they automatically assume it will relate to crazy drama. But in my case, no, I turned the skill of confronting someone into something respectful. Instead of approaching someone with absolute disgust and attitude, I tend to remain calm. I made sure the person I was going to talk to was alone, because avoiding any unwanted attention is crucial. Overall, I was very respectful, kept a great tone, and executed my points all in a way that complimented my character.

Just one person having a positive influence on another person makes a huge difference, that person's mindset has been affected in a way that they pass on to others. As well as that, positive relationships made in the world are carried out daily and productivity in the world increases. We make a different perspective every day in society by influencing others to be and become their best selves.

The 4C's

Today's society is a perfect example of how civility is needed now more than ever. Usually civility is referred to as being weak, but I want to make a point on how civility is the complete opposite.

Remaining polite under hard circumstances, even when tempted to behave out of character, is one of the most admirable things you can do. Since there is a misinterpretation on civility I believe this is why civility is lacking daily in our world. As of 2018, 84% of Americans have experienced incivility and that is an immense percentage. I can only imagine that if these numbers were updated now, in 2021, that it would rise much higher due to current ongoing racism and blatant disrespect, especially towards African Americans. A clear example of incivility was Donald Trump; his speech etiquette was not used in a manner to comfort every audience, but rather only to target the correct rights to one over another.

Due to there being no clear examples of civility, it may be hard for others to understand how to move forward. What tends to be forgotten about civility is that it even includes acknowledging a person's differences while showing them respect. Civility is simply learned over time with trial and error; it's difficult to adjust to a mindset you aren't used to, but it is not impossible. An approach that others can use to move forward toward civility is the golden rule of treating others how you want to be treated. Developing the mentality of this concept makes it easier to live life in an open manner because you then know how to approach situations that may arise for you. Others can move forward by also accepting the reality if they have made a mistake or have done something that was unjust. Since we know civility is learned over time, being able to recognize mistakes and move past them, bettering yourself is proper etiquette for civility. Moving forward with civility should be done unapologetically, meaning that there should be no shame in wanting to do and be better.

Katherine Johnson, Dorothy Vaughn, and Mary Jackson are phenomenal examples of expressing civility. A film called "Hidden Figures" was produced in 2017 that exposed the injustices of racism and sexism in the 20th century and their stories made audiences truly feel the hardships experienced. As I can recall from the film, all three amazing, talented, and smart women went through a major challenge of living under "the white man's rule." Every day as they walked into NASA they would undergo the defiance of white men thinking they are more beneficial and overruled the women's knowledge. Due to the time period, the 1960s, racism was brutal and being an African American woman standing up for yourself in predominantly white male territory was unheard of. These three ladies are leaders and bring such inspiration because, as seen in the Hidden Figures film, white men would tempt these women just to get a reaction and see if they would act out of character. But what is most importantly shown is the civility each of these women pursued. In order to get through the day, utmost respect had to be shown towards these men. It came to the circumstance no matter what, because the risk of black women messing up was major. There was no room to make mistakes and it was evident in the behavior of Katherine, Dorothy, and Mary. For example, since Katherine dealt with math and a calculation might have been wrong from someone else's side, Katherine would have to be so cautious with how she would resolve the problem. It takes a lot to step up in a dignified manner and throughout this time period all three of these women did it. I admire that so much because it takes a lot of personal control and maturity to hold back natural instincts. This all relates to how civility is a learning process and comes from experience because we never truly know what our instincts are capable of.

We can bridge the gap of incivility and civility through continuous respectful, engaging conversations. Being able to talk to that person on a daily basis and address anything is such a beautiful thing. Not only the communication but the comfortableness that you know the other person is paying attention to you and your concerns. It takes effort from both parties, but once that's done anything can be accomplished between the two.

Taking everything into account, civility is a foundation that helps execute all the other Cs; community, creativity, and climate change. Civility builds a genuine and supportive community, creativity is rooted from the actions of civility, and climate change is affected by how we respect our world. All in all, civility is used everywhere and is exemplified in every action we pursue.

Knowing civility's impact is crucial, especially in times like now, to understand a wholesome life, we should all be expressing civility in the purest form possible.

Creating Change for a Better Tomorrow Starts Today

My name is Tamia Louissaint and I'm an 11th grade student at Saint Vincent Academy, where I have received the distinction of Honor Roll for my academic achievements. At Saint Vincent Academy I'm also the Vice President and I help plan, and address the concerns of my peers. I am a National Honors Society student at SVA, as well. Outside of school, I have been dancing for over 10 years with a concentration in gymnastics, jazz, contemporary, ballet, tap, and lyrical. I was also accepted to dance with Debbie Allen in 2018 in LA for a month. I also ran track for my freshman and part of my sophomore year, with hurdles being my favorite event. Additionally, I have been in Girl Scouts since the age of five and am currently still a member and an Ambassador. For Girl Scouts, I have received my Silver and Bronze awards and I'm working on my Gold. I am very active in my church as a youth dance leader. I have choreographed a majority of dances and love helping the girls find their talents. With all this being said, I am passionate about who I will become

The 4C's

and grateful for who I am now and trust this journey I am on with the help of God. My goal in life is to be authentically happy and to enjoy the life I'm living with no regrets. As considered by myself, family, and friends, ultimately I am a positive, supportive, and thoughtful young lady. With my own fashion sense and uniqueness I strive to succeed everyday by expressing my leadership in anything and everything I do.

COMMUNITY

A place, a space, and a feeling. Community is a safe environment where individuals feel like a part of a whole. Each member should feel open to contribute, converse and be appreciated for their characteristics. When we build community we create a bond by building bridges. Community provides a sense of belonging. We are all created with a desire to belong, be seen, be valued, and be loved.

Build community. Build the world – one heart at a time

Dr. Anana

The 4C's

Creating Change for a Better Tomorrow Starts Today

Chapter Five

COMMUNITY KINGDOM CONNECTIONS

Margie Hernandez

"Above all things have intense and unfailing love for one another, for love covers a multitude of Sins (forgives and disregards the offenses of others)." - 1 Peter 4:8 AMP

My mother, Ana, will always tell me how active I was in my childhood years. She always says how easy it was for me to make friends and connect with all types and ages of people. She also said it was easy for me to approach anyone, start conversations, and make friends. As I grew through my teenage years, I was highly active in school activities, sports and clubs.

During my high school years in New York City, I pursued an interest in the fashion industry and worked for many high-end retail stores. I learned many tactics on how to sell, merchandise departments, and window displays. Within the years in the fashion industry, I had established a personal relationship with clients and within my clientele were a few music promoters that offered me a position to work for RMM Records in the promotion department. This opportunity landed me my dream career in the Music Business. RMM Records was a well-known International Latin record company that represented artists like the late, legendary Tito Puente, Celia Cruz, and many more great artists.

One of the qualifications they required for this position was to be bilingual (Spanish). I must tell you a short story; back in my Elementary school days, the school offered the option to attend a bilingual (Spanish) class or an English class and so my wise mother signed me up for the bilingual class and of course I did not want to be in that class. I hated it and begged her to transfer me to the English class and she did not. So, I learned how to read, write and speak Spanish. Thank you, Mom, for not listening to me!!! I would have missed many great opportunities like my dream job. I really encourage you, if you have a chance, to learn different skills or a language – do it! My ability to speak a second language helped me build and establish relationships in my community. You may think you might not use it, but you might be surprised and thankful one day you did!

A Short time after, I went to work for Palma/Baby Grand Records as International Director of Promotion. I worked and single-handedly organized the record label into a viable contender in the Latin market. I had the privilege to work with great Merengue artists and bands. Like the late "Cherito" Jimenez and "The New York Band." I learned the culture and music of the beautiful people of Dominican Republic "Santo Domingo" and learned all the ins and outs of the administration of operating the record company.

Thank you to my Dear friend Dr. Jose "Chery" Jimenez for teaching me everything about the music business, their community and giving me the opportunity to sharpen my communication skills, gifts and talents. I was accepted and thrived in a community that embraced my purpose.

Creating Change for a Better Tomorrow Starts Today

My time working in the Music Industry taught me many great skills and ways to communicate to different types of musical cultures and within that, I also learned ways and how to understand the different areas of the Arts and Entertainment community.

Working with RMM, Baby Grand, Eightball Records, City Sounds Record Pool and Trutone. I also built my networks and relationship within the USA and Internationally with many music peers and Industry Associates and Leaders, Nightclub Promoters and Owners, DJs, Radio Programmers, Producers, Buyers, Distributors, and fans. Having these community connections and networks has also given me the opportunity to freelance and work and help upcoming Independent Record companies in the Music Business.

After 10 years working in the Entertainment Industry, My Lord Jesus Christ blessed me with a beautiful baby girl named Gabriela. As I went into motherhood, I was blessed to be able to be a stay home mom. As my daughter got older, she attended pre-school and I developed a new community as a parent. I became involved with my daughter's school and the Parent Advisory Committee (PAC). I was elected as a Chairperson. Through the years volunteering and serving on this committee, I learned many aspects of the school system. I overviewed the PAC members and parent liaison.

Chaired meetings with parents, teachers and staff. Organized and arranged educational workshops and festivities for the school community. Coordinated annual book fairs with Scholastic Books and made achievements in lobbying for NYC Childcare funding concerns.

As we came together as concerned parents and teachers, we raised a substantial amount of funds through all the book fair events we had. So, we decided to design and implement a parent-led lending library.

The 4C's

We took some of the monetary funds to buy the library furniture, computers and books. This took a lot of commitment and engaging with the school community. We presented the importance of literacy and reading at an early age to our community. It took the entire school community to come together to volunteer every Friday in order to run this program. Community involves people coming together to achieve a common goal. When one wins, we all win.

As I coordinated the recruiting of volunteers my communication skills and marketing skills kicked into gear once again. My vision was to reach every family member, to come together in volunteering and to encourage parents to spend time with their children in picking out books and reading with them. It was a pleasure to get fathers involved and not just the moms. It established a community of fathers, mothers, grandparents, guardians, teachers and staff. We did not exclude anyone because we knew it would take all of us as a community to make this work and benefit our children. Every person was important, and every person offered something. Their skills, experience, talents and gifts provided solutions. We never overlook anyone! This is essential to building and sustaining a community. You should value everyone and never overlook or dismiss others. Everyone that volunteered their time brought something to the perfecting of this parent-run library. For example, one parent worked for the New York Public Library and her experience helped a great deal. She installed and programmed the software and input all the data from each book from the title to the bar code settings. She also programmed the scanners and trained us on how to use them. What a great asset she was for this project. Many others, like her, also brought great skills and qualifications to the program. Every parent and person that worked with this project contributed their time and believed in the importance of the additional enhancement of early age development skills of literacy. Today, I thank the Lord Jesus Christ for allowing me to be part of this experience, that taught me to work within the community of families within that neighborhood and learn from the education community as well. But mostly for the opportunity to be close to my daughter Gaby and be able to be part of her development and growth myself.

A few years volunteering in the Parents Advisory Committee really prepared me in many areas for the next chapters of my life. One of the areas in which it prepared me was how to communicate with this specific area of the community, which was the education area and my neighborhood. I learned the language of the Educators and how they communicate with the parents, children and the community. I also learned how important it is to be part of your children's educational growth and, in doing so, how it brings positive effects in that child's life. Your participation as a parent can impact not only your child but also other children and families, thus the community. I also learned how as a parent you can co- labor with the educators for implementing educational programs and activities that will contribute to the development of the children and it also brings solutions in the areas needed that contribute to your community. Your volunteering and contributions can bring such a great outcome to the school and your community.

My 3 years as a stay-at-home mom and volunteering in the school gave me many experiences and when I went back to work I included the community work on my resume which landed me a position as a Client Manager for WSBA (Women's Small Business Administration) at The Local Development Corp in Brooklyn, NY. There I learned different ways of reaching out to the community.

The 4C's

My job was to communicate and promote all the programs, events, seminars, business classes, workshops, and conduct one on one interviews and counseling with Women entrepreneurs. I promoted and coordinated the Farmers' Market by raising community awareness and attendance for the Local Development. This position also taught me, again, how to learn the language of community developers and upcoming entrepreneurs, local businesses and builders.

When you are called to work in a community you must carry yourself with great humility, dignity and most of all have the love to serve the people in a community. Every contact and connection you make is important within your community. (For example, your home, job, churches, local grocery stores, businesses, schools, doctors' offices, etc.) Even if it does not seem to be connected to the vision or purpose – it's important. Every person you meet from a child to the elderly is important and is a vital member of the community. I highly recommend you always maintain a spirit of humility and gratefulness. Try not to burn bridges with anyone, even if you come to have disagreements or can't see eye to eye.

Always try to bring the peace within any circumstances or chaos that may arise. As they say, you never know if you must cross that bridge again...

"Blessed are the peacemakers; for they shall be called the Children of God" (Matthew 5:9). Amen!

In 2002 after 9/11 in New York City, I relocated to Southern New Jersey. Wanting to be close to my family and concerned for my family's safety.

When I moved to this area, I discovered that there was a high job demand for Bilingual Spanish translators. I worked for many companies, sometimes with no experience, because of the demand for Spanish translators. As I went along, I learned many skills and terminology of interpretations. I became incredibly involved with the community, school, and Spanish churches and served on many boards to find information and awareness offered through social services organizations, community centers, grant assistance programs, children and youth programs, jobs and businesses offered for the residents of my community. I brought the information back to the Hispanic community.

Many people in the Hispanic community were not aware of the various resources and information offered to our community because of the English language barrier. I volunteered my services to help many Hispanic, non-English speaking people in whatever area they needed. I helped with commuting and transporting people to get assistance, writing letters, interpreting letters, assisting in filling out job applications, accompanying them to appointments to assist in translations and even interpreting at church when needed. These skills have been such a rewarding and helpful asset to my community. As the years have gone by my community has brought many great government assistance, businesses and programs and have hired many Spanish speaking employees. It brought great solutions and assistance that increased revenues and brought new businesses.

You see it all comes together in time. My previous experiences and having the opportunity to work in many diverse communities all came together to help others and build the community.

As a born-again Christian now, I have learned that our creator has had all along the plans and purpose with each one of us. In my walk with the Lord Jesus Christ, he has revealed and taught me about his gifts, talents and calls. I thank My Lord Jesus Christ for helping and keeping me throughout the tenure of my life in developing my gifts and strengths. One of the gifts he gave me was the gift of an exhorter and all throughout my life I was walking, operating and functioning in this gift to build communities.

I highly encourage you to seek the Lord to reveal your gifts. The Lord does not want you to be ignorant about this. Each one of us has a gift. Your talents will operate in every area of your life and throughout your life and your gifts are given to you to use and to help others and serve your community.

"A man's gift makes room for him and brings him before great men" (Proverbs 18:16). Amen!

I exhort you to write down the visions and dreams the Lord has placed inside of you. Do not give up no matter the circumstances.

Pray for the proper alignments, kingdom mentors and connections!! But most of all, the most important connection you can ever have is a relationship with the CREATOR of the Communities, our Lord and Savior Jesus Christ!! Amen!!

"But seek ye the Kingdom of God, and his righteousness; and all these things shall be added unto you" (Matthew 6:33). Amen!

Creating Change for a Better Tomorrow Starts Today

Margie Hernandez, was born and raised in Brooklyn, New York. Her parents are both Spanish nationalities. Her father, Jose Gonzalez, is from San Jose, Costa Rica and Her mother, Ana Gonzalez, is from Barceloneta, Puerto Rico. She is the mother of one beautiful daughter Gabriela Montalvo, 24, and grandmother to three handsome grandsons, Luke Gould, 7, Joseph, 3, and Ryan, 1.

Margie Hernandez has invested 20 years of her life in working in New York City Limelight of the Entertainment Business from Fashion to the Music Business. Learned all the aspects of Administration, Retail, Distribution, Radio, Clubs, Artists Promotions, Sales, Management and Entrepreneur.

Moving from New York in 2002 to New Jersey, she had a personal encounter with Jesus Christ and was saved in 2004. In the beginning of her walk and her new life in the Lord she encountered and birthed her prophetic gifts and her calls. In 2015, the Lord took her International to assist in helping to promote a 3-day Prophetic Conference in London. In this trip the Lord connected and opened doors and she got to witness the many Prophecies come to pass!

The 4C's

Amen! The Lord established many kingdom relationships throughout the years in her walk; she made many Kingdom contacts and relationships. "To God be the Glory" Amen.

Margie Hernandez, an entrepreneur, is in the future planning on establishing her Kingdom Connection Agency, Promoting Music Artists, Authors, Media, Organizations, Businesses and Events. Presently she is the Manager of Streaming Música in New York and working with Dr.

Anna Phifer of BlessedGirl organization.

Chapter Six

COMMUNITY REQUIRES COMMUNICATION

Aaliyah Smith

There are 4Cs: Civility, Community, Creativity, and Climate Change. My "C" is Community. I bet you are wondering when I think of the word Community, what I think of. Maybe you are wondering how I would define a community. For me, there are many types of organizations and companies that make up a community. Some of the things that come to mind when I think of the word community include family, groups, neighborhoods we live in, where we work, people, and experiences. The length of time and exposure within those communities contributes to our overall experiences.

Naturally, some of the groups I am involved in are based on my parents' decisions such as the church I attend, where I am part of the youth group and church usher group. Although my church is a group that I was born into I enjoy my church family. At my high school I participate in subgroups such as the dance team, Black Student Union, JROTC, and Latinas United to name a few. Each one of those groups create opportunities for me to grow and learn more about myself. Girl Scouts is the group that I am most active in. I have been

The 4C's

in Girl Scouts for about 8 ½ years and also hold a position in a subgroup called Teen Leadership Circle.

Although my involvement and length of time in each group varies, each group is important to me, and I feel like I belong. The community that you are in should always make you feel safe and supported. You should never feel like the community you are a part of is trying to change you. Make sure the community groups you participate in are trustworthy and supportive. The positive connections you make will last a lifetime.

The impact that my C has on my life has been challenging at times but exciting. While the opportunities are great there have been times where I have stretched myself too thin and had to rethink my plan. There are many different experiences that I have had the opportunity to be involved in. These groups have made a lasting impact on my life. I have learned new skills and many lessons and met a lot of people along the way.

I was a student at a private school and that experience allowed me to apply for and was selected to meet the Governor of Kansas. I was allowed in her office and took a picture with her. That particular visit to the Capital I was also a page for the Senate for the day. I met many lawmakers and saw the discussions that take place on the floor and experienced different sessions. I was also able to meet the mayor of Kansas because of my involvement in student government.

My parents also encourage me to volunteer my time outside of my groups. My mom signed me up to volunteer at the Department of Veteran Affairs. During this volunteer experience I served some of our nation's veterans. My responsibilities were to give out clothing and sort donations. I, otherwise, never would have seen first-hand how our veterans need our help and support after they have served our country.

As I mentioned earlier, Girl Scouts are a big part of my life. The mission of Girl Scouts includes getting girls to step out of their comfort zone. I definitely have stepped out and don't seem to be as soft spoken as I was. I have represented my troop on many occasions and was selected to meet the national CEO of Girl Scouts. I have done so many things from selling cookies, volunteering at domestic violence shelters, food banks, and decorating graves at the National Cemetery for Veterans.

Girl Scouts has taught me many skills over the years such as business, organization, communication, and leadership. I have seen many opportunities to do more and be more come my way, my job is to be prepared.

Often I think of how my community has helped me overcome many obstacles in my life. For example, if I am struggling to meet the goals I want to achieve that day, I always feel comfortable enough to ask questions or seek any type of help if it is needed. My communities l help me keep a positive mindset, and motivate me to not give up when it is hard.When I think of leaders in the community there are many that come to mind.If I had to choose just one I would have to say my inspiration comes from Dr. Ruben West. He has inspired me in many ways by showing dedication and working hard at everything he puts his mind to. He is known all over the world for inspiring others to give their best and be their best. His personal initiatives are similar to the one I am working on for my Community Poultry Project. He is working to build up communities by bringing joy and inspiration to them.

Dr. Ruben West has created several successful businesses and encourages others to do the same. If there is something that needs to be done, he rolls up his sleeves and jumps in to help. I can always count on him to be there when I need him. He may not think I am paying attention to him, but I do. I hear him say "Live Your Best Life and Do It Now. Why? Because you only get one!" Dr. West makes me think I can do anything and be anything that I put my mind to. I have partnered with him on a few projects and can't wait to see what the future holds. We have a lot of traveling to do!

The COVID-19 Pandemic has affected my communities in many ways and has been extremely hard to deal with! I have been confined to my home and restricted from seeing my family that live in the same city as I do. In order to deal with it I started setting up weekly Zoom calls so that we can all see each other. That has helped somewhat but we are still limited on face to face communication. Since in person learning has been restricted, I have been participating in online learning for the past year now. I missed a lot of school activities as a freshman. I never thought I would ever miss attending school every day but, I am ready to go back!

During the spring and fall I normally get a chance to volunteer at the Black Belt Speakers conference that is hosted by my uncle. For obvious reasons both sessions had to be canceled. Hopefully, this year it will be scheduled again now that we have a COVID vaccine.

I have not had the opportunity to be very active in the communities I am a part of with face-to-face contact this year, which has been difficult. I'm sure you can imagine how hard it is to participate in Girl Scouts virtually. My family and I also had several places we were planning on traveling to, but unfortunately we had to cancel those plans.

The places I would usually volunteer have to take precautions to protect the residents. Those under 18 are not allowed in their facility. It has mainly been hard for the people who have lost their jobs, their homes or for the families who experienced a death in their family from COVID. While I have several things that have negatively impacted my community because of COVID I am grateful that I am still here.

Seeing the COVID-19 Pandemic unfold made me realize the vulnerability, racism, and injustice that exists within many communities. We all know that there has been a lot of racial tension and feelings over the past year. Minorities, supportive individuals, and companies have become more outspoken about injustices. The negativity is not new to our community, but it is now viewed in real time due to technology. It is easy to see that we lack empathy, compassion, forgiveness, and equal treatment for all. There have been multiple events over the past year that have shown the true colors and feelings of different communities and groups within. There is a big difference between a peaceful protest and a riot. Unfortunately, there are those that like to put the two in the same category to keep confusion going. Some people don't see the need to have these conversations or acknowledge the truth.

When I think of the United States, I would have to say this country is too divided. There are some really hateful and mean people in the world. It makes it hard for communities to move on if they can't be treated equally. We all need to grow up, own up to our mistakes, and try to make the world a better place and put all of our differences aside. The world is full of different races and ethnicities but, we were all created by God, and we all have a purpose on this earth. It may take longer for us to realize what we want to do with our life, but God will lead us to it.

The 4C's

Communication is one of the necessities for positive community interaction. Social media allows you to communicate with your friends, family, and community. It is also used to keep up on current events and some businesses use it for advertising. I feel social media is a necessary community; however, our elders don't see it that way. Our elders believe that kids spend too much time on social media. You always hear them say things like go outside and play, read a book, or do something productive. They think we are lazy and spend too much time on our phones, whether we are talking on the phone with our friends, surfing the net, or texting.

It is essential to have social media now. I have seen schools use it to communicate information to parents via Facebook and Instagram. It is also a platform to learn and launch business ideas or personal initiatives.

I currently use Facebook, Instagram, and Snapchat. My other forms of communication are email and standard text messaging.

I feel like we can bridge the gap with social media, if we all have an open mind about all of the different opportunities the platforms bring. The first step to bridge the gap begins with adults explaining their concerns about social media and their social media rules.

Many adults say "no" or "because I said so." This creates a bigger misunderstanding between youth and adults. Social media is one of the most critical communities we have at this time. This is proven by how we have been forced to use social media to handle business over this past year during the COVID pandemic. For instance, we now use social media to stream church, work, school, and other meetings.

Social Media is a powerful communication tool. I use it to promote my Girl Scout Gold Award called the Community Poultry Project. Let me tell you about my Community Poultry Project (CPP). This project will be completed as my Girl Scout Gold Award, which is taking place right now in Kenya, Africa. My goal is to empower women of the community and build their self-esteem. I believe that everyone deserves to have access to the same resources such as water, food, a warm place to stay, and clothes to wear.

This project will teach participants how to be self-sufficient, self-sustaining, and give them bargaining power via poultry. Many of the single mothers have limited job and business opportunities in their local area. It will also give them a commodity to generate income. Families, mostly those run by a single mother, experience food insecurities on a regular basis. This project will give them the ability to have food as well as tradable resources for other edibles. This project will teach knowledge, skill, and business principles that can and will be passed from parent to child.

My ultimate goal is to create a program that can be duplicated in many different areas. With that, this will give others the ability to have the money to pay for their family's expenses. They will also eventually use some of that money to start a business of their own if they want to. With their business, they would have the ability to have a sustainable income and a way to keep providing for their family. They then can keep passing down the business for generations to come. Therefore, I am continuing to document every step, to share with the next community.

I have already teamed up with several quality people that will help make this endeavor successful. I have a team in the US which helps with raising the funds and marketing my project. The team in Kenya serves as my boots on the ground and are the direct eyes and ears of what is happening. All of the team members will be volunteering their time, which will in the end provide thousands of dollars' worth of value.

In August of 2020 I hosted a Zoom groundbreaking ceremony. This provided an opportunity for the donors to see the area for CPP and meet some of the people of the village. I introduced my team and allowed them to have words to express the passion they have for the CPP project. As a leader it is important to identify the strength of each of your team members. Everyone adds value and we will use our positive energy to build this community.

Although the Community Poultry Project has a team in place we want to provide opportunities for the men of the community as well. The men of the village are the construction crew. Since the terrain is so rugged it makes it impossible to deliver the supplies directly to the site by vehicle. Once the supplies are unloaded off of the truck, the construction crew walks the supplies to the site. They are also limited on the construction equipment, so they use heavy tools to break the rocks by hand. Allowing the men of the community to work on the project gives them a sense of brotherhood and purpose. This is an additional component that has given the men of the community the jobs to provide for their families.

The Community Poultry Project will hold 500 chickens easily! This will provide more opportunities for the women of the community to share in the responsibility of the ongoing needs of the project. They will provide care and oversight of the facility once it is up and running. We are taught in Girl Scouts how to give communities that are forgotten hope and increase their sense of self-esteem by creating opportunities they never thought would be possible. This

Creating Change for a Better Tomorrow Starts Today

project has helped me think outside the box and create a global impact. I will also continue to establish relationships around the world to promote positive change. Girl Scouts is about empowering girls and what better way than to create opportunities for them to build wealth for themselves and their families.

Some may ask me why I chose to start a project in another country. I answer their question by saying; nothing is stopping me, so why not? Everyone deserves a chance and it is up to us to find a way to help them. I realize this is not an easy project and other Girl Scouts aren't taking this route. That is completely okay with me. You see I wanted to do something that was a real challenge for me. I never want to be like the next person, I march to my own beat. I am determined to finish what I started. The people in the community are counting on me. I can't wait to see the completion of this project. I plan on traveling there this summer, so I am praying COVID is out of the way.

As a teen I am learning more about myself every day. My project is giving me a chance to improve my leadership and communication skills, which will be used in other areas of my life. I'm learning to listen to the needs of the people. I believe they will not only tell you what they need but they will show you where you can help.

On my honor, I will try: To serve God and my country, To help people at all times, And live by the Girl Scout Law. I will see this project to completion.

To learn more about the Community Poultry Project please visit my social media pages. Be sure to click like. Comment on the post. Share with those in your community.

The 4C's

Facebook

Community Poultry Project Makueni County, Kenya. You can also view my web page: cppkenya.com

Instagram

CommunityPoultry_Project

Please consider donating to my project. All funds come directly to me and are monitored and released by my parents.

CashApp Tag: $GoldCPP

Creating Change for a Better Tomorrow Starts Today

Aaliyah Smith is a transformative and spirited leader with progressive experience and substantive results in program and project management, investigative research, quality control, and process improvement. She is exceptional at program planning, implementation, and assessment capabilities supporting multiple simultaneous projects within a complex teenage environment.

Aaliyah is capable of translating vision into initiatives that improve team engagement and ultimately performance. Senior Girl Scout Aaliyah Smith of Kansas is currently a sophomore in high school. Aaliyah is working on her Girl Scout Gold Award in Kenya, Africa. She has a true passion for helping and serving others.

Aaliyah is a member of the high school dance team, JROTC, Black Student Union, and Latinas United. She also holds a position with the Girl Scout Teen Leadership Circle, Aaliyah has hundreds of volunteer hours and is active in her community. She likes shopping, traveling, and spending time with her family and friends when possible.

CREATIVITY

Is for the brave-courageous risk takers. Creativity is for the problem solvers. Your ability to be transparent and authentic with your ideas is powerful. Creatives are the rule breakers, the ground shakers. Tap into your imagination and create the change.

Dr. Anana

Chapter Seven

CREATIVITY: EXPLORING NEW IDEAS

Simone Banks

Let's get one thing straight, your mind holds no limits, period. When you think of creativity, your mind wanders to art, music, or entertainment; things that are pleasing to your senses. Creativity isn't just about thinking outside the box, it's also about exploring new ideas that are different from everybody else's. It's about seeing new, effective ways to tackle problems or shape the world we live in. It's about pushing through the norm and expressing how you feel via your ideas, your work, the way you talk, walk, and the way you view life as a whole. It's about dreaming, and letting your mind run wild without limits. About letting your thoughts, feelings, and words wander freely without a level headed master. However, to me, it's just about coming up with new ways to be better, to translate your ideas into something that you love.

I never thought of myself as a creative type of person, plain and simple. I'm your regular run of the mill high school student. I get average grades, I like to cook, and draw, listen to music, and every now and again read and write. I'm a hopeless romantic, a human dictionary, and described by my peers as a poetic idiot. Now when I describe myself like that, and look at me on the surface, there's not

The 4C's

much to talk about, is what I thought. It took me a long, long time to realize this but I am not a level-headed person in the slightest. There have been times where I just sit down and do nothing but think. There's no exact thought, I just let my mind wander and do whatever it wants to do. And the pictures that my imagination crafts are beyond wild. Sometimes they're fun, other times they're action packed, dramatic, sad, or goofy.

The stories I create in my mind are filled with emotion and passion; they have well thought out characters. I can see them speaking, moving, singing, dancing, crying, laughing, and being spontaneous. I know their backstory, their feelings, and their personality; because it all comes from me. I confuse myself with all of the stories and gimmicks that I come up with without even really doing anything. I translate what I see in my mind into something that everyone else can see; whether I write it, sketch it, or say it. You don't need blood, sweat, and tears to create something that can be considered creative. You don't need a topic, an idea, or an example; all you need is your imagination. There will never be a wrong way to create something, as long as it comes from you. A single thought is all you need to spark an entire adventure or a tale of epic proportions beyond your wildest dreams. One word can ignite the path of greatness; a journey of your own creation.

There's a phrase that's been engraved in my memory ever since the beginning of elementary school, "Don't judge a book by its cover." That phrase has been my personal mantra for some time. On the surface, it states to never judge somebody or something on how they look. It's often used for one's physical appearance, and even sometimes to describe a person's mental state. But, I've always thought about that phrase when it comes to making art, specifically drawings. I draw a lot, and one day I hope to become a famous cartoonist. I may not be able to draw everything, or be the best at drawing humans, but what I do draw comes solely from my imagination. However, everything I create is often misunderstood by others. Some say they're cute and cool, others say they look weird and ugly; which, I can understand, not everybody thinks the same way I do. They'll never understand the way I think, and that's ok. But, what really makes me mad is when people only judge what's on the surface. They give what they see one thought, and that's the end of it. Thinking twice is not an option in their mind, there is one option and one option only.

Trying to explain what you draw is almost never easy; for some it's like trying to speak backwards. But I truly despise it when people judge your art style, which happens a lot to me. I love the way I draw and wouldn't change anything about it. Granted, it would be nice to pick up a few more skills, but all and all, I take pride in my cartoons. However, I'm often asked to draw things that are beyond my limits. I'm told that I should take lessons to get better, or that I should change my art style, or practice, or just get better. Don't get me wrong, taking art lessons isn't a bad thing, neither is practicing; but you can't just completely change your art style. The way one draws is their own, it's theirs, and you shouldn't change it because it's special. Coming into your own as a better artist doesn't just happen overnight. Yes, it's always nice to practice to improve your skills, but to change the way you draw entirely just because someone else didn't like it? Your creativity blossoms through everything you make and changing that completely wouldn't make your drawing yours anymore; a backstory with no character, lyrics without music, a god with no purpose, a masterpiece without a signature. The way you create something is what makes it creative in the first place, because you're making something that is only coming from you.

The 4C's

Your ideas, your thoughts, your feelings, your emotions; everything] that dwells deep within your mind, spirit, and heart.

Critics say that art can be interpreted in any way you want. It has no true definition; it only means what you truly want it to mean. I personally don't believe that this is entirely true. Every drawing I make, every character I create, every animal I draw has a backstory behind it. Whether it is a tale of achieving your dreams, or being tough as nails, or being misunderstood. All of my cartoons have a definition, they possess a personality, and thoughts, and feelings, and emotions. But I've been told time and time again that I'm drawing something from my heart the wrong way. I will admit, I am incapable of drawing everything, but I always know when I push past my limits. My answer to bystanders who criticize my passion is, "It's not that I can't, it's that I choose not to." My creativity is all in my imagination. I can interpret anything into my drawings; whether it's humans, animals, landscapes, or goofy cartoons. They may not look like what other people think is normal, but as long as you believe it looks like what you imagined, then it's perfect. Creativity and imagination go hand in hand, they can spawn, create, destroy, or give meaning to anything you can imagine. Your mind holds no boundaries, and your only limits are what you believe they are.

Creating Change for a Better Tomorrow Starts Today

Simone Ellen Grace Banks is 14 years old and resides in Edison, New Jersey. She is currently a Freshman at Edison High School where she is a member of the AVID advancement college program. To date, in her educational career, she has received the humanitarian award for generosity and kindness.

Simone is a seasoned member of the Perth Amboy, NJ of NJ Orators. As an orator, Simone has spoken at rallies such as the Black Lives Matter protest given by the Rays of Hope Foundation in Jackson, NJ and has expressed her views abroad at the Live Your Best Life London Global Youth Initiative Training at the University of Westchester in London. In addition to being an orator, Simone is also a member of the New Generation Teen Choir and the Dance Ministry at the Cathedral International in Perth Amboy.

When Simone is not in virtual school, she enjoys cooking, gaming, singing, sketching, and writing. Simone hopes to become an accomplished cartoonist when she gets older. Simone is a proud member of BlessedGirls.

The 4C's

Chapter Eight

DARE TO BE CREATIVE

Omaiah Hall

What does creativity mean to me? Creativity is the way I take my trauma and mold it into an art form; it's the way I thrive when I sing a song or dance center stage. Creativity is the way you solve problems, communicate and the way you use your imagination; when researching what creativity is, these were the terms that constantly kept sticking out at me.

The purpose of this chapter is to share my experience as a creative, who I am and how the arts have helped me and molded me into the person I am today, how the arts literally saved my life. Growing up I have been surrounded by musicians and dancers, but even though I've been surrounded by them none of them made me feel like I could make art a career. My mom's a dancer, my father a pianist, and many other family members are singers and musicians; this thing ran through my veins, but it wasn't just a hobby for me, like it was for them. I wanted to make this my career then and I am making this a reality now, to become someone that puts Guyana on the map for the arts. Growing up my family included me in everything, piano lessons, dance classes, choir even modelling training to keep me occupied and out of trouble. They invested so much in my art growing up because they saw my passion but never verbally said that I could do this as a career and always doubted me, which made me fear coming out as an artist.

Years passed and it was just a hobby as far as my family was concerned. I never voiced my dreams but I certainly did push and say that this is something I may want to do. They took it as a joke and I was ok with that because I understood the concern, because in Guyana it's hard earning money as a creative; it is difficult, but what I didn't get was the lack of support. As time went by I started pressing on it and got involved so much more with the arts, not just practice, but I finally decided to take it to the next level and actually study it. I wrote the exams and not just passed but was one of the best Theatre Arts students for my year. That solidified in me that this is what I want to do with my life. Arts is my passion, my escape and it deserves to be respected in my country and I want to bring that respect.

I sat my mom down one evening for the first time and we went deep into conversation about my future and what I wanted. This first time she still didn't completely get it but we met in the middle deciding I could do art and pursue another career. This was one of our first real conversations about my future and for us to meet somewhere was phenomenal. Why I am saying all this is to really show that things will never always go your way but with compromise you can get what you want, and if you come from a family that doesn't quite get you and your creativity it takes a lot of talks and conversations. After a year we had another conversation and now I am applying to an arts school in the Caribbean pursuing my dreams with the support of my family. It takes time but with communication it's possible, if you want something you go for it and fight.

Creating Change for a Better Tomorrow Starts Today

The arts saved my life. How you might ask. You know when people say use your art to express yourself? I used my art to fully express who I was then and who I am now. In high school, the color of my skin and the texture of my hair bothered me; the figure I carried triggered my insecurities. I told myself for 3 years straight that at the age of sixteen I was going to bleach my skin because I felt ugly. One day I sat in my room crying for hours, at the age of fifteen, and wrote a song; I never released it, but it was for me to remind myself of my beauty. There is beauty in everyone; ignore social media, ignore the haters – there is so much beauty in you.

That's a bit off track. I wrote a song and sang it to myself for days, feeling that energy for days, then weeks and I no longer wanted to make any drastic change; your girl moved from being timid and allowing every little thing to get to her to being loud and aggressive and forceful for the right reasons. My art saved me. I took that time to cry and write, expressed myself the only way I knew how and it saved me. This is one of many because today I am still struggling with my identity, still fighting my inner pain, but when I write and let all that out it calms me. I say all I want to on a piece of paper, whether in the form of poetry or song, and perform it for myself and right then and there I am reminded of how powerful I am. The year 2020 wasn't an easy one for many of us, but my creative juices were flowing because of all the pain I felt. It may sound sad but it saved me. I was stressed about online school, I was fighting with myself and my relationship was killing me slowly because I was too afraid of the truth. I cried for weeks, stopped eating until one day I poured my heart out into some beautiful pieces, the pages held my tears and that saved me. I was this close to giving up but I couldn't let the world miss this beautiful piece of art that came out of a painful setback.

The 4C's

Being a creative is powerful, we tend to stick to ourselves mostly and use our art to share who we are; we tend to stray away from the world and live in our own imagination and that's ok, that isn't a bad thing; I know people think it is but it isn't. Your therapy is your art, whether you sing, you dance, whatever it is you do because being a creative takes many forms, but as long as you stay true to you and you pour your heart out into your art you can be unstoppable. You pour it into your art and let the world know who you are, or you pour it into your art and you let yourself know who you are.

Funny story: I was not allowed to write Theatre Arts at the High School I attended, back in 2017 I was fighting to write it, but I failed at convincing them. You'd think that would stop me. I went to another school to ask if I could write just this one subject through them, with the help of my arts teacher we pushed and pushed and I wrote it. I thank God daily for allowing me to have these gifts, but also placing creatives in my path to succeed. Not only did I pass but was one of the top students for Theatre Arts that year, and only God could've done that because when one door was closed I fought my way for the other to be open.

Creatives, I will forever preach this: dare to be no one else but you, be brave, be bold, be absolutely you. Use your art, your creativity to touch yourself and there will be others looking on and saying this is who I want to mirror, this is the person that inspires me to be my true self. By being you, the world cannot stop you. The world may try and it can get hard sometimes, but after the storm time smoothly and beautifully passes by. Dare to be creative, dare to be you.

Creating Change for a Better Tomorrow Starts Today

I am nineteen years old and my name is Omaiah Aaliyah Hall. I was born Guyanese. I am a second year communications student at the University of Guyana and a young pioneer of the Arts in my country, Guyana. I am a singer, dancer, model, poet, songwriter and hopefully, within the next few years, a Professional Arts Practitioner using my talents and skills to better the arts of my nation. Guyana's Junior Calypso Monarch 2019, the founder of The BeYOU Community, and a top 5 delegate of The Miss Guyana Teen Scholarship Pageant 2019. Within my chapter you will learn more about me, and my trials as an artist, what I have done, what I desire to do, and the many mini achievements in between. My hope is that any creative reading this never gives up, stays true to themselves, and pushes hard for what they want.

The 4C's

Chapter Nine

DON'T BE ORDINARY, BE EXTRAORDINARY

Karina Brown Known as – KTA

The definition of "Different" is not the same as another or each other; unlike in nature, form, or quality. The definition of "Creativity" is the ability to transcend traditional ideas, rules, patterns, relationships, or the like, and to create meaningful new ideas, forms, methods, interpretations, etc. Let me show you how emotional pain led to my creativity. I always had creativity in me, even as a toddler. The first thing I did as a creative person, was to be a dancer in a West African Dance Group at the age of three. I was highlighted as a featured dancer because of my high intensity and passion for dance. As a toddler I would dance solo in front of thousands of people. No one knew that I had a secret. I had an undiagnosed issue that greatly impacted my life. The first five years of my life I was literally living in my own world because I couldn't hear anything, but I had a bulky amount of love for music. No, I couldn't hear the music, but I did feel the beats. Nobody in my family knew I couldn't hear because I had mastered reading people's lips early on. My Mother found out I couldn't hear anything when I was five years old because she was talking to me one night in the family car, and I told her that I couldn't hear her because I couldn't see her face! I asked her to turn around because I couldn't see her lips. After the circumstance of me not being able to hear people and things around me, my whole family came to the realization that the reason I'd hold strong eye contact with people and the reason I had always ask for the music and TV to be turned up extra loud was because I didn't have the ability to hear people and things around me.

The first time I got my hearing aids, it was the best day of my life! I could finally hear! The first thing I did when I got my hearing aids was turn around, with my mom behind me, and I asked her to speak. I asked her to speak because I wanted to see what it was like to hear without looking at the mouth of a person. I was so excited, but I didn't think of the consequences, I only thought of the positive things about me being able to hear. It was only a matter of time before I started seeing how it really was to be hard of hearing in a world full of negative and ignorant people. The first 6 years of my life, I thought the world was Rainbows and Unicorns. I thought everybody was nice like the people in movies. I thought I was going to have lots of freedom, no violence, and no negativity. After I turned 6, I started slowly seeing the real world. I started seeing people doubt my creativity and my intelligence. The first person to doubt my creativity was a close family member, someone I thought would support me forever.

I'm a self-taught artist, meaning I haven't had professional classes but instead I teach myself how to perfect almost everything that I've drawn. As a young girl, I would draw specifically only cartoon characters, Tom and Jerry, Popeye, and Olive Oyl, The Flintstones, etc. After I got kind tired of drawing cartoon characters, I tried to teach myself to draw people. My biggest mistake was trying to teach myself how to perfect people in front of that close family member. I was hard on myself because it was one of the first times where I'd draw something and waste more than two pieces of paper, so out of frustration I said, "I can't draw people." After I said that they didn't even hesitate to say that if I can't do it then I can't do it. I don't know what I was expecting them to say, but it wasn't that at all. I didn't believe in myself for a long time after that incident. Almost all the other adults believed in me, but one negative voice can be louder than thousands of positive voices. How was I supposed to believe and trust what people say when not even my own family member supported me? I went back to drawing cartoons for three more years and would draw people without a face every now and then.

The same year that I was told that I couldn't draw faces, my family and I moved to a new house, and my Mother got sick. I was only six, but I was also one of the only people who took care of my mother. Taking care of my mother was harder than I thought, but I never left her side. I didn't notice, but I started overeating and I was also beginning to become less patient. I was gaining weight rapidly and slowly becoming sadder. I was mean to other people because I didn't want them to be mean to me. My mother healed after seven months, and then I switched schools.

I was still overeating and was still mean at first, but then I became nicer which made things worse for me. Once I started being nice, more people started being antagonistic towards me. I wasn't accepted in the "abled" community, they always talked about how I speak differently than the other kids and would mock me for my voice. I wasn't accepted in the "average body" community, I constantly got belittled just because I was heavier than a lot of students. I also wasn't accepted in the Non-POC (Person of Color) Community, I was constantly reminded that I'm a black girl in America everywhere I went. All of this made me feel like I was anything but human. My self-esteem got worse and I couldn't believe that I could do anything. There were a lot of adults trying to tell me that I needed to ignore them, and a lot of my friends saying why would I let people who look like that, (they were basically calling them ugly) talk about me. But words really do hurt. Words ring in my head and they make themselves heard repeatedly. I always tried to convince myself that maybe it was my revenge for being mean in the first place, but then again, I never straight bullied people, I only rejected people and made them not want to be my friend. I regret being so mean and bitter because I really started seeing the true and dark colors of people and of the world. I know I was going to end up seeing how the world is anyways, but it's like I regret being mean because I think that was my revenge but at the same time, I can't help but think that if I had kept being mean maybe I wouldn't have let them belittle me. The more people showed hostility towards me, the more sensitive I became. I mistook being sensitive for being weak because I always cried whenever something negative was being said to me. I hated how sensitive I had gotten. But now that I look back to me being sensitive, it all adds up that being sensitive took me to the right path. Little did I know that my sensitivity would only make my life better and help me see the world differently. Because I was so sensitive to negativity and being different, I had a passion for people who were different and who were treated differently. I had a passion for people specifically with vitiligo, which is a condition in which the pigment is lost from areas of the skin, causing whitish patches, often with no clear cause. I also have a passion for people with albinism, which is a condition where there is a congenital absence of pigment in the skin and hair and the eyes. The passion for people who were different was always there, but I started showing love towards eccentric people publicly by painting the beauty of Vitiligo and Albinism. I paint them to show people of those conditions that they are beautiful just the way they are.

The first time I knew I had a love for people who were different was when I had a blind friend in elementary school. I loved him a lot and I would do anything for him, and he would do anything for me. We were the best of friends until we lost contact. He appreciated me because I was nice to him and I treated him like he was human because he was and still is human. Being treated differently made me realize how other people who were treated the same way felt. Finally, I had realized that I should treat people exactly how I'd like to be treated, with respect. How could I talk about getting respect from other people if I'm not respecting other people? My passion for Vitiligo started when my mother introduced me to one of her friends who has the condition. It was almost a love at first sight type of thing because I thought her skin was just so beautiful. I always knew the condition existed, but I only saw it on TV, never in real life. After seeing vitiligo in person, I decided to bring it to my paintings and drawings. I didn't really think about who it would help or anything, I just knew that vitiligo and albinism were both beautiful. People who are different were not the first things that I painted; I've been drawing since I was three years old, and painting since I was 9 years old. I can't remember the very first thing that I drew but I do remember that when I first started painting I painted mostly Black angels and praise dancers and then some were just Black people. But now I paint celebrities who are activists and I paint people embracing their culture and much more.

The reason I make all black art is because I want to show people that I'm very comfortable in my race and skin tone. I went through a phase where I didn't really know about who I was. I wore braids for a protective style but whenever I would wear my hair naturally it was always straightened and permed but the only reason I let that happen is because I hated my natural hair. I hated how thick my hair was, I hated summertime because I didn't want my natural hair to be revealed. Because of the humidity, I just hated my hair no matter what. I started really wearing my natural hair when I was in the 9th grade, and I guess it was out of the norm for people. There were people who complimented it but there were also people who told me to "do my hair" and that I needed to "comb my hair" and sly comments like that. I did let it get to me at first but then I came to the realization that they probably won't even be in my life in ten years so why should I care what they think. I decided to just wear my hair out no matter what people might say, and I gained more and more confidence. I am proud to say that I've never hated my skin tone, I probably never hated my skin tone because my mother always made a point to compliment the color of my skin whenever she could, and she reminded me that she prayed for God to give her a chocolate baby. I appreciate her so much for that.

My mother always taught me that the best revenge is success, and she's never been wrong about that. The success I've had so far has probably been my best revenge. My favorite revenge is that I have some art pieces around the country of America. It may not be many, but the fact that more than one person outside of my state and city has something that I created makes me feel so good inside. My first success started with being a vendor in my own city. I didn't sell anything, but just the fact that more than people from my family or staff and students from my school saw my art, made me feel so good I really didn't care whether I sold anything or not. My second success was also being a vendor, but this time it was a little outside of my city and I sold two paintings! It was the next best day of my life. My third success was having my first art show; I had over one hundred paintings and I had about one hundred people come see me and my art. By my third success, I had concluded that I would go by KTA, also known as Karina the Artist, whenever I'd go somewhere to represent my art. My fourth success was going to the Worldwide Vitiligo Conference in June of 2019. As a vendor there, I was in heaven! That was my favorite success because I met the most awesome and kind people there.

They treated me with the utmost respect and I treated them with the utmost respect. I met people from Greece, Turkey, Jamaica, and all over the World! My fifth success was being the first teenage solo artist at my local public library for the Pierian Group, which is an international group that appreciates and celebrates Master Artists. It was such an honor. All of these happened before I turned 16 years old.

Truth be told, there were some challenges between all that success. The same close family member who started off being unsupportive and really tearing me down, suddenly, wanted to act like they really cared about my artwork and what I was up to. They started asking questions about why I didn't paint the faces on my people even though they are the reason I didn't do faces in the first place. They wanted to show up and act like my manager at the big events but behind closed doors they were still uninterested or negative.

They also always focused on the financial piece, like how much money did I make? Although they never offered to support me buying supplies, it was very frustrating. I brushed it all off because I knew if they really did care about me and my passion, they would know that I'm not doing art for money and they would know that KTA stands for Karina The Artist. I didn't really care about what they had to say, all I cared about was how my mother was holding up.

My mother was sick four years in a row from 2014-2018 and then she got sick one more time in 2020. It didn't really have any effect on me until 2020. The reason it frustrated me the most that year is because it was the same year that I was displaying my art at the library. The hardest part wasn't even the fact that I had to take care of my mother, it was the fact that I had to talk to all the adults about my art myself, my mother usually does a lot of the talking for me because she usually has all the answers and talking to people isn't something, I like to do a whole lot. When I do talk to people, it's usually something positive or a question. I don't want to self-diagnose, but 2020 was the year where my voice was belittled the most and my social anxiety had gotten worse. My voice was belittled by both adults and young adults. People had talked about my voice all the time, but 2020 was the year that it crawled on me and that it kept being mentioned. People were saying things like "you sound different" or "why does she sound like that" and other things as well. I felt like it was totally uncalled for, especially since whenever it was mentioned I was interrupted when talking. My anxiousness didn't get worse until the pandemic. I avoided everybody for at least 4 months. I stopped going to a checkout with a cashier and did just self-checkout instead, I was ignoring my friend's calls, I even avoided contact on social media apps. I'm grateful to have the friends that I have, though, because they understood completely why I wasn't talking to them. Even though the pandemic affected me in a negative way, the pandemic also affected me in a positive way. The pandemic helped me with my creativity, and it made me feel more comfortable with being me and doing things that my insecurities would never let me do. Wearing shorts and wearing tank tops during the summer was one thing that changed for me. I never liked revealing an ounce of my body because I wasn't comfortable in my body. I mean I was so uncomfortable in my body that if I could cover myself from head to toe year-round I would. Another thing that changed for me – I am creative. I'm way more creative and I had more time to tune into my creativity and not just painting or drawing either. My creativity has expanded with cooking, makeup, and dancing.

Being creative literally comes in all forms. Creativity has changed the world. Creative people have invented everything we use in the world today. It takes a creative person and a creative mind to come up with any ideas at all, honestly, so I guess you can say almost every individual has some creativity. Some people just prefer not to show that side of themselves and some have not discovered that side yet. Being creative isn't easy, though; some people have it in them but just don't want to display it and that is okay because being creative isn't the only talent in the world. As a matter of fact, being creative can come with some challenges. Being creative can lead you to thinking that you don't fit in with anybody or that the world is just too bland for you or that you are too much for this world. You can control your creativity and allow it to take over you, or to take over only part of you. Being creative and being different are two different things but can work together in certain circumstances. Being "Different" would be like if you're so creative to the point that a lot of people wouldn't understand your creative thinking or only a certain audience will appreciate your creativity. Examples would be someone like Lady Gaga, Beyoncé or Nicki Minaj; a lot of people think their styles are weird or different but there's a certain age group who appreciate their creativity. And being "Creative" would be like where you are creative enough for this world to accept you and your art. An example of a creative enough person would be someone like Rihanna; people think she's a genius and that she's creative, but not eccentric, (or at least that's what I've heard). One unique woman who inspires me is Eunice Kathleen Waymon also known as Nina Simone. She inspires me because she stands out when it comes to her singing voice and her essence. She has one of those "don't care about your opinion" flows that I just absolutely love. She also uses her singing/creativity to display her activism. Being an activist during her time, I can imagine would be much harder than being an activist today. So many people approved of her singing voice but not of her race. She was different but that never stopped her from being successful or thinking that she could be successful.

The point I'm trying to make here is that there is always going to be someone who doesn't appreciate your existence in this world but there is also always going to be people who do appreciate your existence in this world. Just be yourself, the only person whose opinion should really matter when it comes to you is your own.

There will be days where you feel like you don't like yourself and days where you feel very confident in who you are but those are normal human feelings. And that is what all of us are, human.

Thinking about how I am literally human and how I am going to have feelings and that it's okay to express them, is one of the ways that I got to where I am today. I didn't come up with that conclusion that I could have feelings alone. I have someone by my side who has guided me through the challenges and hardships, which is my mother. Finding the right shoulder to cry on is like trying to find the perfect shoe. It takes time to find your person.

And it takes time to find yourself, too! But you will get there. Stay dedicated, never give up and success will be yours and that's a promise!

The 4C's

Karina Brown, is a teen phenom that is cutting a path to fame through her fresh and unique approach to art. Born 16 years ago, Karina was a unique child with a bubbling personality. At 3 years old she began drawing and perfectly sketching/duplicating whatever she decided to draw. At the age of 5, Karina was diagnosed with a significant hearing deficit that resulted in her being fitted with hearing aids. Immediately, she embraced her new normal and began educating her peers about hearing loss and how to interact with her. As time progressed her skills increased, she would accept challenges to draw Old School Cartoons, like The Flintstones, Jetsons, Mickey Mouse, and multiple Disney characteristics. Since the age of 9, she has focused on Acrylic paintings, challenging herself to perfect eyes, noses, and various body parts. Over time this self-taught artist has developed her brand. As she matriculated through school, she encountered bullying because of her "difference" of wearing hearing aids. This painful period increased her sensitivity to others who are treated differently. The canvas became therapeutic for her. In 2016, she became intrigued with Vitiligo, the autoimmune disease that causes discoloration of the skin. Her passion and curiosity lead to her doing a series of Vitiligo Art, showing the beauty of the individual patterns. For her, the uniqueness of the patterns is walking art and she sees God's beauty in each pattern. She has been a vendor at local events but proudly presented her "Gallery" of over 60 paintings at her formal Art Show on September 21, 2018 at the tender age of 14. In October 2018, she attended the Live Your Best Life Jr. Black Belt Speakers Conference in Kansas City. Her paintings were sold and taken back to North Carolina, Kansas, Texas, Florida, etc. She set her sights on attending the Vitiligo Conference. Her dream became reality when she attended the Worldwide Vitiligo Conference in Houston. During the conference, she was interviewed by Fox25, the local television station because of her passion and interest in the disease. The video has been seen nearly 60,000 times. Karina is personable, humble, passionate, and humorous. She looks forward to expanding her art displays and promoting her motto "BE EXTRORDINARY, IT'S OK TO BE DIFFERENT!!"

Her Personal Statements

- I started drawing at 3 doing cartoon characters and graduated to painting at 9.

- I am a self-taught artist who has never had an Art class. I taught myself to draw eyes, lips, and noses.

- I am hard of hearing and wear devices to help me hear; therefore, I know how it feels to be different. My paintings represent differences so that people can see the beauty in their differences.

The 4C's

- Most of my paintings come with a blank face because I want people to focus on the meaning of the paintings not just their eyes.
- My favorite type of painting to create are the ones with famous civil rights activists or poetry addressing social issues.
- I have a goal to build a beautiful African American Art School that provides training that is free or very affordable.

Chapter Ten

CHANNEL YOUR INNER CREATIVITY

Quanisha Patterson

"Creativity is the bridge between imagination and reality" (Quanisha Patterson). The aforementioned was a quote I painted in black and white on a coffee smelling page of my unofficial journal when I truly grasped the essence of Creativity. It perfectly describes this subjective term as Boden (1994) termed it. How is Creativity subjective? As Gardner (1994) posited, "No person, act or product is creative or uncreative in itself. Judgments of creativity are inherently communal, relying heavily on an individual's expertise within a domain." Essentially, Gardner defined creativity as a distinctive way of finding a solution to a predicament given that this solution is valued in various cultural settings. His belief impacted an agglomeration of discussions and criticisms as he raised awareness of the various levels of intelligence and creativity and furthermore, the correlation between intelligence and creativity.

According to the Oxford Dictionary, Creativity is the use of imagination or original ideas to create something. Therefore, Creativity is an exceptional concept which seeks to explain the formation of either a tangible or intangible item from a mere idea

The 4C's

obviously stemming from one's imagination. As Blythe expressed, it is the ability to develop and express ourselves and our ideas in new ways. This is definitely so because Creativity enables us to think "outside of the box" and experience a new version of life.

Creativity is found in a number of disciplines inclusive of psychology, humanities and even sociology. When scrutinizing Creativity from a Sociological point of view, it is clear that Creativity forms a relationship between individuals and society since relationships can change the culture of society through creative thinking. Oftentimes, persons misconstrue what creativity is by believing that persons are only creative based on what they do and that creativity can never be developed. However, mere occupation can never limit a person's creativity and, as a matter of fact, creativity is developed at any point in time. Hence, Creativity has various components and forms and is not just limited to "Creative Writing" although it is usually thought of in that aspect.

Creativity has five main components as proposed by Sternberg which are expertise, imaginative thinking skills, a venturesome personality, intrinsic motivation, and a creative environment that supports and refines creative ideas. Similarly, the Wright brothers suggested that creativity has four main ingredients inclusive of space, time, trust, and play. What exactly did they mean? Whether your office or even your bed, ideas definitely need room to develop and what is the space without the time given to develop?

Additionally, the fear of failing is inevitable but to combat that fear, trust is required and even when you trust yourself, you must "play" (experiment) to make your dreams reality! From simply analyzing those components and ingredients, the fact that creativity is extensive is reiterated and it is now "duck soup" (undemanding) to identify some forms of creativity.

To what extent is Creativity in our everyday lives? Simply adding an extra ingredient to your soup or even inventing your own recipe is Creativity. We are Creative daily, sometimes even subconsciously. Other common forms of Creativity include Poetry, Arts and Craft, Dancing, Acting and Music, amongst many other activities.

On a personal level, Creativity is a fundamental aspect of my life – integrated in both my leisure and professional spheres. However, in both aspects, Creativity is never used in a monotonous way for me and this makes me have a deeper appreciation for this trait. It encourages me to have an idiosyncratic perspective not only on life but also on my predicaments. "Creativity is the way I share my soul with the world." These words of Brené Brown will always be profound because they are so ideal! Bred and buttered in the confines of the only country in South America with English as the official language, I am an 18-year-old International Poet, Actress for Lloyd N' De Arts, Entrepreneur, Egalitarian, Award winning Painter, and Ambassador for Just Keep It Natural and Sach.

Generally, Creativity enables me to pacify anxiety by exhorting optimism, expressing myself, coping and even solving tribulations. Being in the Creative Arts Sector as an International Poet and Co-author to various books, I am encouraged daily to persevere and it indirectly keeps me spiritually grounded. Moreover, Creativity has enabled me to effectively continue my self-love journey. How you may ask? I have found creative solutions to enhancing my self-esteem through the use of Poetry as my method of catharsis and self-love by my perusal of uplifting books. Creativity has caused me to evolve into an even more inspirational young woman to fellow youths of today by instilling positivity, determination, faith, uniqueness and bravery into me.

Every type of Creativity definitely instils unique traits in us but obviously intersections will be present. Upon perusing recent receipt of the George Simon Prize for Junior Visual Arts - Folklore Edition 2020, I realized that just by painting "The Sovereignty of Ol' Higue," patience was implanted in me as a long-term characteristic. Additionally, as an actress and Ambassador for various companies, open mindedness, expressiveness and punctuality alongside various other traits were fostered.

The true beauty about Creativity is that it isn't forceful. Hence, all the lessons learnt will be long term and not short term because to truly learn those lessons, the "intrinsic motivation" and "venturesome personality" as aforementioned, must be present!

However, given the worldwide concern of Covid-19, the ballgame has transformed for many creatives – mainly in the negative light. It came with an agglomeration of demerits with merits being the silver lining of every cloud of demerits. However, it is with a cheerful spirit that I say, I was, without a doubt in the selected few that chose to use the Global pandemic to yield positive results.

Being a firm believer of faith being "the substance of things hoped for and the evidence of things not seen" (Hebrews 11:1) and always maintaining a positive outlook on life, many opportunities were proffered, and I even used this phase to develop new skills and perfect my crafts.

Consequently, the pandemic definitely has enabled me to become more tech savvy and way more open-minded when forming creative solutions. One such example of this is the enhancement of my way of presenting my poetry and branding myself on my social media platforms. Due to the pandemic and the development of technological skills, my creative juices are now even more extensive and as such, I now use graphic designing to aid in the remarkable appearance of my pieces.

Despite using the pandemic to my advantage, the heart-rending effects are observed especially from an Entrepreneurial view. In the antecedent paragraph, my Entrepreneurial title was vaguely mentioned. Hence, details will now be given. I am the sole proprietor of my online bakery, namely, The Q-Plan. When a person is the sole proprietor of a business, there are a multiplicity of obligations, inclusive of the formulation and implementation of ideas, which, in Guyana, are all susceptible to being purloined.

With the existence of the pandemic, matters have only worsened due to heightened desperation causing a densely populated market and a surge in "Copycat Culture." Moreover, it is quite ironic that copycat culture is used under the guise of creativity and innovation.

Copycat culture refers to the stealing of ideas from one business to be used in another. This culture is extremely discouraging for creatives especially in Guyana because of the lack of protection for intellectual property. With this, I do implore the Government to implement Intellectual Property Laws or Copyright Protections so that the thin line between inspiration and blatant stealing will never be breached again. Moreover, Private or Public Organizations may host Entrepreneurship courses so that persons may learn the credentials of becoming a successful entrepreneur rather than freelancing and purloining ideas which enables a monotonous market. However, to immediately appease the situation,

The 4C's

Entrepreneurs should brand their work and take necessary precautions to prevent becoming susceptible to this tribulation, for example: when posting a photo, a logo can be engraved to prevent other entrepreneurs from utilizing that photo on their social media platforms.

It is important to take necessary precautions to prevent parasitical practices. It is extremely agonizing that the copycat culture isn't the full extent since today's culture is generally consumed by trends and band wagons. Therefore, I believe that genuineness or authenticity is missing because oftentimes people decide to commence projects or simply start an account on a new social media platform because others are doing so and not because they genuinely want to. Even in the Creative writing sector, many persons choose to write or create for popularity and not because they authentically love the Arts. Henceforth, persons are unwilling to step beyond the norms of culture due to the fright of being shunned by many.

Therefore, persons are so petrified to have their own opinions or trust their intuitions and rely solely on validation from others. This creates a virulent space for creatives to dwell and needs to be terminated immediately. Why not take a note from History? We should be inspired by the many people that impacted creativity!

Just take a look at Walt Disney's empire built entirely off of his imagination or even Newton's discovery of Calculus! What about Einstein's inventions of the gas absorption heat pump or the refrigerator? The true essence of creativity was captured by these brilliant minds and had a long-lasting impact on the world!

With high hopes of sharing my creativity with the World, there are a few projects that I am currently developing and actively working to complete. Firstly, as a member of the Kupanda sisters that proselytizes literacy in Guyana, by partnering with the World Literacy Foundation. We have commenced aiding students from Sophia's Primary School and due to the pandemic, many hiccups were presented. However, we are constantly working on various ways and means to continue supporting students. Nevertheless, I've decided to take matters into my own hands and donate not only books to pupils but also offer to do sessions with them. The idea to host sessions with the students primarily stemmed from hosting Creative Writing sessions with students of various age ranges as the Vice President Head of Creative Writing of the Bishops' High Schools' Arts Club.

As the President of the Bishops' High Law Society, aside from weekly sessions, a Career Workshop is being established as well as an Easter Charity Drive for the less fortunate. Additionally, on a personal level, I plan on releasing my first book soon and hosting my first poetry workshop to enlighten people from all walks of life about the importance of Poetry as it is the language of the soul. It is important for us, as a nation, to realize that Creativity plays a fundamental part of our lives by aiding in appeasing trials and tribulations through innovation and an open mind. When society begins to lose its Creative spark, it will become close minded and this explains why body shaming, racism and injustice amongst many other societal issues still exist, because we are close minded. Furthermore, many of these issues stem from poor socialization in the homes and schools. There are numerous ways that both parents and teachers stifle creativity in children especially by expecting perfection and discouraging any form of leisure. Moreover, as Dr. Meri Cummings suggested, creativity is killed when parents or teachers force children to always complete activities, or do anything for that matter, one way which they deem "the right way"; this discourages these children from taking any creative risks. I think a misunderstanding between parents and children today is the thin line between youth asserting independence and being disrespectful. I undoubtedly agree that some teenagers or youth may be disrespectful but others simply would like the liberty to make certain decisions, for example; the occupation they are desirous of pursuing.

Frequently, many parents try to live their lives through their children by neglecting how their children feel. A child may desire to become a professor but the parent is dissatisfied and forces that child to become a neurosurgeon. It may seem like an infinitesimal issue, but quite frankly, it is not because that child may become emotionally disconnected from their parent by feeling neglected and unappreciated. Furthermore, to cope, he or she may resort to undesirable remedies. On the other hand, some parents may simply be encouraging their child or children to put their "best foot forward" and children may perceive this as the parents trying to control them and may actually become disrespectful as opposed to asserting independence.

What is a problem with no solution? To bridge the gap and learn from each other, I believe communication definitely is key because misunderstandings are bound to happen due to the generational gaps. Relationships should definitely be established between parents and offspring to offset any predicaments and have a general understanding of each other.

"Creativity is experimenting, growing, taking risks, breaking rules, making mistakes and having fun." (Mary Lou Cook). If you take away nothing else from this chapter, take this away: Use Creativity as your guide! Allow Creativity to help you engage your mind and understand yourself so that you may develop non-linear thinking and nurture confidence. Let Creativity instill empathy into you and give you a voice to advocate for yourself and others so that societal issues will decrease! Always remember: "Creativity is not a competition" (Autumn Sky Hall).

Channel your inner Creativity!

The 4C's

Engulfed in the Caribbean, bestrewn with meaningful experiences in the land of many waters, Guyana. Quanisha Patterson is an 18 year old International poet, Entrepreneur, Egalitarian and Youth Advocate amongst many other proficiencies. Educated at various institutions, inclusive of the New Guyana School, Success Elementary and currently, the Bishops' High, she pursues an Associate's of Arts - Law Degree with the aim of securing her Bachelor's and Master's degrees soon.

Within her educational experiences, she has demonstrated remarkable leadership qualities with not only the earning but maintenance of exceptional positions. In the Bishops' High, Quanisha has contributed to two focal clubs tremendously – The Bishops' Arts Club and The Bishops' Law Society – and was also a lead singer in the choir. In 2019 - 2020, at age 17, she was awarded Journalist and Treasurer of the Arts Club as well as the Lower 6 Representative and Assistant Public Relations Officer of The Law Society.

Succeeding that, she currently is the Vice President, Head of the Creative Writing Department and Public Relations Officer of the Arts Club as well as the President of the Law Society. Earning these positions was no surprise to the public after Quanisha gained qualifications of 17 subjects with 8 grade ones, 8 grade twos and 1 grade three and was furthermore deemed the best Additional Mathematics student, best Home Economics student, best Clothing and Textiles student, best Theatre Arts student and best Electronic Document Preparation and Management student – all in the year 2020. Additionally, she was selected for Youth Parliament in 2018, received legal training at the Ministry of Legal Affairs, and was a member of the winning team of the Innovation challenge at the Queen's College Student Conference STEM fair in the aforementioned year. Moreover, she is computer literate and has completed all her courses and was awarded certificates from Global Technology Inc. and even exceptionally represented her school in a Video Competition on Gender Based Violence by Guyana Responsible Parenthood Association earning a book voucher with her colleagues.

Aside from her studies, Patterson partakes in many activities inclusive of leisure pursuits. As mentioned earlier, she is an Entrepreneur because of her recent establishment of her bakery, namely, The Q-Plan. Additionally, she is the manager of her family business while also continuing her studies. Furthermore, she is a spoken word artist and has performed for many events inclusive of the Miss Cultured Guyana Pageant 2020, Pakaraima- Guyanese Canadian Writer's Association, the University of West Indies' Mental Health Open Mic Night, and was even a Drama Festival Finalist for Spoken Word 2020. In relation to her poetic career, she has two individual articles and a few published pieces, one of which, to be precise, "The Sovereignty of Piece," aided her work in seeing the limelight making her an international poet through its publication in the World's Biggest Anthology 2020.

Additionally, she is the co-author of "Trapped in Thought" and aids in the promotion of literacy in Guyana as a member of the Kupanda Sisters which partners with the World Literacy Foundation and she even contributes to the education sector through the provision of poetry for the simplification of content for the Caribbean Examination Council.

Quanisha is also a member of the Girl Build Girl Foundation, Co-author of BlessedGirls 4Cs Anthology, Brand Ambassador for Just Keep it Natural (a natural hair company) and Sach (skin care company), and she was even featured on various pages inclusive of the recently established Female Empowerment page. She commenced writing as her method of catharsis but now she incorporates societal issues to raise awareness and encourage youth to utilize their talents in her quest to make a positive change! She also played instruments inclusive of the drum, recorder, steelpan and guitar and is also an actress, artist and yogi.

Her artistry was showcased in her winning piece "The Sovereignty of Ol' Higue," which earned her the George Simon Prize for Junior Visual Art, the Guyana Annual 2020 Folklore Edition. Playing an integral role in various productions is also in her track record from acting for "Theatre Reload" and "March Montage" to being a member of the Public Relations team for the House of Pearson's Fashion Show. She is now a member of Lloyd N' De Arts Company after being awarded the best Theatre Arts student in 2020 from this company and is also a Fashion Enthusiast, Tutor and Counselor.

Creating Change for a Better Tomorrow Starts Today

With a rigid spiritual background and an empathetic spirit, Quanisha continues to weather the storms and encourage others to do the same as she paints beautiful smiles in every room her steps are engraved.

"Dance in the night and you'll never be afraid to fly in the light." - Quanisha Patterso

The 4C's

The Q-Plan

Creating Change for a Better Tomorrow Starts Today

CLIMATE CHANGE

Global Warming and Global Climate Change. We must consider culture change to identify and break old habits that harm our planet. Climate change is an existential threat to our future. Understand your connection to the climate and how we are globally connected. There are small changes we all can do to impact climate justice and restorative justice.

Ring the alarms – the house is on fire! Let's listen, live and learn how to save the planet.

Dr. Anana

The 4C's

Chapter Eleven

BURUNDI FACES THE EFFECTS OF CLIMATE CHANGE

Gatumba Village Case

Globally, climate fluctuates for a variety of natural reasons for instance, more recently, the "Little Ice Age" and the "Medieval Warm Period" occurred (IPCC report). Burundi has not failed to experience the impact of climate change as well. Burundi is a country located in East Africa that is divided into five ecological zones.

Burundi has abundant water resources with good rainfall. The forms of energy consumed in Burundi are wood and charcoal, which represents 95.3% of the overall energy balance. Natural ecosystems include forests, savannahs, bushes, low meadows, and marshes and other aquatic environments, most of which are distributed in 14 protected areas with an area of about 157,662.85 ha or 5.6% of the country's total national area (Paul, Jane Olwoch, Tom Downing, Jillian; April 2009).

In our case, Gatumba village was suddenly affected in April, 2020 by floods which to date the inhabitants are still destabilized. Their investments, economic setups, social relations, progressive education, family relations, and spiritual growth, just to mention but a few, have been negatively affected. With merciless results of living in the internal displaced refugee camps where life is a mess with poor health conditions, distorted family and marriage privacies, women and teenage girls' sexual abuse, immorality, and discontinued education among many others.

Effects of Climate Change in Gatumba

The village of Gatumba lies on the western side of Burundi, near the border with the Democratic Republic of the Congo. The village has been experiencing floods due to climate change since April 2020 and the habitat in Burundi remains precarious and fragile.

According to ©*UNICEF Burundi/2020/Z.BOUJRADA* report, "*it all happened overnight. On April 19th, 90% of Gatumba's population lost their belongings to the river. The small city, just outside Bujumbura, sits by the Ruzizi river. With the heavy rains and the water flowing down from the hills, 10,000 households lost their belongings overnight. As a result, 11 out of 14 schools in the district have suspended classes: the schools are flooded, and the buildings are at risk of collapsing.*"

Economically, the population of Gatumba lives mainly from agriculture and petty trade. The fields (beans, corn, tubers) have been under water since April 19. The ones living on petty trade, who were already barely surviving because of the DRC border closing due to COVID-19, have witnessed the little they still had been washed away by the water.

Gatumba faced increased vulnerability under climate change and rising costs of climate risks significantly. This extreme flood decreased the long-term growth by reducing its annual GDP significantly. What is more worrying is that future climate change may lead to a change in the frequency or severity of such extreme weather events, potentially worsening impacts; in February 2020, heavy winds attacked Gatumba village and the neighboring area of Kajaga which extended Lake Tanganyika's waters to business areas and tour sites, affecting their daily businesses. Impacts are likely to have disproportionately strong effects on the poor as such vulnerable groups have fewer resources to adapt to climatic change.

Discontinued education has greatly affected the children and those who didn't get help from well-wishers are still in the refugee camps today not knowing if they will ever manage to go back to school and recover all that was lost. Four (4) basic schools suspended classes because they were flooded or because they were being used as temporary shelters for displaced families. Pupils have also lost their school materials.

The 4C's

Families' investments and relationships have been greatly affected because of the loss of their homes, house belongings, and dignity all over to sudden floods. It's a trauma that needs support but not limited to spiritual, psychological, economical and giving a helping hand to bring them back to the life they used to live, if not better.

Among the many needs left unmet are shelter; Burundi Red Cross assessment reports show that 504 homes were destroyed and are uninhabitable, 589 houses were partially damaged, and 1,041 houses were affected. Livelihoods and basic needs; the displaced population is experiencing food shortages due to loss of livelihood, low purchasing power, and disruption of markets. In terms of food access, displaced families rely on one meal a day for both adults and children. In normal situations families feed twice a day. Other needs are protection, gender and inclusion, water, sanitation, hygiene and health.

Creating Change for a Better Tomorrow Starts Today

Over a thousand people have sought refuge in the official site developed in Kinyinya II. They need everything: shelter, access to water, hygiene and sanitation services, food, medical care, alternative education for children, child protection, and psychological care for traumatized persons.

Jane Wanja Kamau

Kenyan volunteer missionary in Burundi since 2012. Founder and program director

Burundi Community Outreach Missions (BCOM).
www.burundioutreach.org

Ambassador Blessed Girls - Burundi @February 2021.

Professional Background

Certified Public Accountant (CPA) Part 1 Higher Diploma in Business Management

Bachelor of Art in Theology in Christian Ministry

Experiences

Exportation of fresh cut flowers to FloraHolland Auction markets

– 6 years in Kenya and 1 year in Burundi.

Working with International Institutions – Universities, Primary & Secondary schools – 4 years in Burundi.

International volunteer missionary – 8 years.

Chapter Twelve

CLIMATE CHANGE: OUR CRITICAL ASSIGNMENT

Landra Richardson

Discussions on climate change might not be as refreshing as a cup of icy water for most people. Still, it is urgent to attend to, like an assignment you haven't started but is due the very next day. Imagine the feeling of extreme anxiety that kicks up your body temperature, causes an addled mind, and profuse sweating. The suffering desire to complete the assignment so your body systems can cool off from the adrenaline, stabilize, and adequately function might be a simple depiction of what our world is slowly undergoing. Climate change is our critical assignment that's due the very next day; put on your thinking caps because "We are the first generation to feel the effect of climate change and the last generation who can do something about it" (Barack Obama, Former US President).

Whenever you listen to the news today, you hear about two things, the pandemic and global warming. Even though the pandemic is front and center of everything, the concept of global warming has not lost its importance in the scheme of things. Over the past several years, and with more frequency during the last few years, experts have been calling for everyone, including you, to note this phenomenon and give it the attention it requires. The reason being that it is the cause of climatic changes that lead to detrimental chaos. Scientists have produced evidence that the planet has been heating up at an alarming rate. The earth is now at the highest heat level it has ever been in 800,000 years. The international community has come together in response to the scientific evidence presented and has signed accords relating to each country's schemed efforts to limit and ultimately decrease its contribution to the phenomenon. International pressure has also been brought to bear on countries deemed to contribute to global warming without any demonstration of seeking to address the situation.

On the other hand, many skeptics, like Jim Inhofe, scoff at the idea that the world is heating up to the degree that would destroy life as we know it and cause irreparable harm to the planet. They point to the fact that there are places that are experiencing record cold weather and posit that these pockets of increased cold weather are proof that the earth is not heating up as much as the proponents of global warming are claiming. In the face of these arguments, which are indisputable, since the same scientific evidence records increasing and more acute cold weather even in places that have never experienced snow and cold, the most logical question one can ask is, "Who is right? How can there be global warming when some places are getting colder?" We then have to ask ourselves, "What exactly is global warming?" and the follow-up question, "What is the relationship between global warming and the cooling down experienced by some regions?"

The answers to these questions and a better understanding of the coexistence of both warming and cooling being experienced at the same time are found in the fact that there are two separate yet related phenomena taking place at the same time. These two phenomena have been erroneously linked together in some circles, but scientists have identified them separately. They are described by scientists as global warming and climate change. **Global Warming** refers to the rise in global temperatures due mainly to the increasing concentrations of greenhouse gases like carbon dioxide in the atmosphere. **Climate Change** refers to the increasing changes in the measure of climate over a long period of time, including precipitation, temperature and wind patterns.

NASA describes climate change as, "encompassing global warming, but referring to the broader range of changes that are happening to the planet. These include rising sea levels; shrinking mountain glaciers; accelerating ice melt in Greenland, Antarctica and the Arctic; and shifts in flower/plant blooming times." This means that the two phenomena are considered to be different even though the terms describing them are sometimes used synonymously. The increased cold weather is attributed to climate change while the increased planetary heat is attributed to global warming.

Global warming was not recognized as a phenomenon until Svante Arrhenius, a Swedish scientist, posited that the combustion of fossil fuels could lead eventually to enhanced global warming. He theorized that there was a direct relationship between atmospheric carbon dioxide concentrations and temperature. Arrhenius measured the average surface temperature of the earth at 15°C (59°F). This was due to the natural greenhouse effect; which is the effect of water on the concentrations of carbon dioxide. He believed that if the carbon dioxide emissions were doubled the temperature would increase by 5°C. He along with Thomas Chamberlin deduced that human activities could warm the planet by the addition of carbon dioxide to the atmosphere. This prediction was not given much attention because it was believed that human activities were insignificant in comparison to natural forces. The oceans were thought to be able to cancel out human pollution of the atmosphere because they were able to absorb great amounts of carbon dioxide.

In the ensuing years more research revealed that there was an upward trend in average temperature. In 1976, Stephen Schneider predicted global warming (Maslin in Lenntech). However, the term was not officially used until geochemist Wallace Breckenridge of Columbia University wrote a paper entitled "Climatic Change: Are We on the Brink of a Pronounced Global Warming?" (Columbia University). The term was then accepted into the scientific lexicon. Up to that point the changes in temperature were called "inadvertent climate modification" because even though scientists accepted the fact that human activities could cause climate change, they had no idea what direction that change would take. They understood that aerosols – tiny particles of industrial emissions – might cause cooling, while greenhouse gas emissions would cause warming. Nobody knew in the 1970s which effect would dominate. So it was accepted as a modification.

Global warming finally got real attention and became a dominant topic in June 1998 when NASA scientist James E. Hansen testified to the United States Congress, "Global warming has reached a level such that we can ascribe with a high degree of confidence a cause and effect relationship between the greenhouse gases and the observed warming."

Scientists were finally able to convince enough governments that the planet was heating up at an alarming rate and that it did not bode well for the future of civilization. In the last half-century, the average global temperature increased at the fastest rate in recorded history and, according to the experts, this trend is accelerating.

NASA records show that all but one of the sixteen hottest days in its 134 recordings have occurred since 2000. "The powers that be" began to take notice along with the media and Non-Governmental Organizations and global warming became a part of the conversation in mainstream society. It was no longer just a science problem. It was now shown to be a societal problem with international ramifications.

The main cause of global warming is the increase in greenhouse gas emissions. These gases, however, do not magically appear in the atmosphere. It has been discovered that humans are responsible for 95% of the increase in greenhouse gas emissions on the planet, resulting in increased levels in the atmospheric temperature. The Intergovernmental Panel on Climate Change, a United Nations group of scientists, in its Fifth Assessment Report stated that there is a 95% probability that human actions over the past 50 years have warmed our planet. It also stated that the industrial activities modern civilization depends on have raised atmospheric carbon dioxide levels almost double in the last 50 years. That is why global warming focuses on the increase in greenhouse gas emissions caused by humans. Research shows that natural atmospheric greenhouse gas emissions maintain a planetary temperature that is almost constant and accommodating to plant and animal life on the planet fluctuations occur at a rate that allows the planet to correct itself. The gas emissions from human activity causes spikes in the atmospheric temperature that are so acute that scientists do not believe that the planet would be able to recover if measures are not taken to remedy the situation, with urgency.

Global warming, or the "greenhouse effect" as it was called, takes place when certain gases in the earth's atmosphere trap heat. These gases let the light and the heat from the sun into the earth's surface; this energy is absorbed and then released back into the atmosphere as heat. Greenhouse gas molecules trap some of the heat and the rest escapes into space. The greater the amount of greenhouse gases in the atmosphere, the greater the amount of heat that is trapped. This naturally leads to greater warming of the atmosphere. This is why it is called greenhouse gas because it operates under the same principle as the agricultural greenhouse. It lets light in, but traps heat.

There are a number of major contributors to global warming, although each of us has contributed, and continues to contribute to global warming. One of the biggest contributors is the burning of fossil fuels. The industrialized nations are guilty of this as they burn fossil fuels to make electricity. In the United States alone fossil fuel burning produces around two billion tons of carbon dioxide (CO_2) per year. This staggering statistic is from a country that has rules governing the environment. The Environmental Protection Agency oversees the regulations that were implemented to protect the environment from harm or destruction. This number is increased exponentially if we are to factor in the other industrialized nations like China, Russia, and India that are only now making baby steps in terms of trying to reduce greenhouse gas emissions. We also need to include the other European countries and, to a lesser extent, the developing countries of the Third World.

Americans' second-largest source of greenhouse gas emissions, and by extension those of the other developed and developing countries, is transportation. The transportation sector generates 1.7 billion tons of carbon dioxide each year. Again this is from a country that has regulations governing the state of vehicles that are licensed to be roadworthy. Emissions from vehicles in the other countries will be astronomical. The coal and oil being burnt causes oxygen in the air to be combined with carbon thus making carbon dioxide and increasing carbon dioxide concentrations in the atmosphere. There are many other sources of heat-trapping pollutants. The commercial agricultural industry releases vast amounts of chemicals and fertilizers into the atmosphere. Chemical plants also release pollutants into the atmosphere despite the existence of regulations barring this practice. Deforestation is another major contributor to global warming. Large logging companies cut down trees without any thought to environmental impact. This behavior takes away one of nature's most effective controls of carbon dioxide. Trees regulate the presence of carbon dioxide in the atmosphere. Large-scale farming also destroys the rainforest as large swathes of land are cleared for farming. This is made even worse when the forest is burnt so that farms can be established. This contributes to global warming in two ways; it destroys the rainforest thus robbing it of its ability to regulate the carbon dioxide and at the same time it releases more pollutants into the atmosphere through the smoke from the fire. The Amazon rainforest is a good example of this state of affairs. It has been burning to a greater degree each year as more and more cattle ranchers and commercial farmers move in to establish their Enterprises. According to a NASA study, humans have increased atmospheric carbon dioxide concentration since the Industrial Revolution.

Global warming is a topic that should be of the highest importance to every person on the planet because it will eventually affect every person, if it has not already done so.

The 4C's

Global warming will affect every aspect of our civilization and every facet of society. If it is allowed to continue at the rate at which it is going, then civilization as we know it will no longer exist.

Some of the effects of the phenomenon include the following:

❖ On average, the earth will become warmer. Some areas will welcome warmer temperatures, but others might not. These warmer conditions will more than likely lead to more evaporation and precipitation. However, it might vary with some areas becoming wetter while others become dryer. There will also be more and more prolonged heat waves and more powerful hurricanes.

❖ The greenhouse effect will warm the ocean water causing it to expand. It will cause glaciers and ice sheets to melt thereby increasing sea levels. This will lead to widespread flooding. Flooding will cause destruction of private property as well as public infrastructure which will place a financial strain on both government and private citizens. Flooding could also lead to the transmission of sickness and disease and even lead to dramatic water shortage.

❖ The increased temperature also has the potential to cause an increase in wildfires. Some of which we have already witnessed in the United States and Australia.

❖ Global warming can lead to droughts as we have seen in various parts of the world, especially in the African nations. Drought leads to crop loss which leads to poverty, hunger, and even starvation in some cases. However, the problem then becomes an international problem, which will further strain national economies. Since this will be a planet-wide situation, there will be a point at which the richer countries will not be able to help the others.

❖ Climate change can cause new patterns of pests and disease, which are a danger to plants, humans, and animals, to emerge. These can pose new risks for food security and human health.

❖ Because of the increase in air pollutants and an increase in pollen-producing weeds, allergies, asthma and infectious diseases will also increase. Again this will be an added financial strain on families and governments.

❖ Destruction of habitats will cause some species to become extinct. This will affect us in ways that we do not yet know. What we do know is that we are all dependent on each other. (U.S. geological survey 2021)

The potential effects listed above have a direct bearing on every individual and family on earth. Food shortages, the destruction of infrastructure, new diseases, storms, and shortage of finances will affect life as we know it. It will put a strain on marriages and family life. Jobs will be lost, people will become desperate and angry to the point of a breakdown of law and order. This is the reality of global warming on the micro-scale.

Fortunately for our civilization the world leaders have begun to understand the seriousness of the situation and have taken steps to avoid the fallout from global warming. On April 22, 2016, one hundred and ninety-five leaders from around the world signed the Paris Climate Agreement. In signing the Agreement they pledged that they would implement strategies and legislation to assist in making the goal of the conference a success. In other words, they were going to work from their individual nations to try to limit global warming to below 2 degrees with a preference of 1.5 degrees.

Most of the countries were true to their promise and began to put legislation in place to lower greenhouse gas emissions.

However, it's a long hard road to the end of the journey because it means that people will be called upon to make changes to their lifestyles and businesses will have to change the way they interact with the environment. This means that they might lose some profit and for a business that is never a good option. The big oil and coal companies along with large chemical plants will not want to give up their monopoly of the fuel industry. They will not go quietly into the night, even if the alternative is a disaster. So we have a long way to go in order to get to the goal.

In the meantime, we as individuals can do our part to erase our carbon footprints. We can start with little things like saving water and using less electricity when possible. We can also plant a tree. Small steps, but every step counts.

In spite of the fact that some people believe that global warming is a hoax, the evidence is sufficient to prove that global warming is indeed a very real phenomenon and the forecast if it is allowed to continue and increase is not very encouraging.

Global warming is an indisputable fact.

Creating Change for a Better Tomorrow Starts Today

Landra Anatha Richards

Landra Richards is a final year undergraduate at the University of Guyana, pursuing a Bachelor's Degree in Biology. She wishes to better understand biodiversity and how we can influence it's change for the better. She is a co-editor and co-creator of the

M.O.V.E. (Mangrove Operations and Volunteer Equities) in Guyana as well as a fourth year representative of the University of Guyana Bio Club. She collaborates with local animal rescue organizations including ARAPS-Tails of Hope & Paws for a Cause. She continues to participate in mangrove restoration and clean up projects and is working towards developing an aesthetic, sustainable and long lasting dish bowl from coconut endocarps.

As a multi-potentialite, she has established skills and passions in multiple aspects of life. She pioneeres her own kids community yoga sessions, she is a personal yoga instructor/trainer for kids, an athlete, artist, writer, and model at TraitsManagement.

The 4C's

She hopes to build a network of unified minds that are invested in similar interests. Her goal is to serve herself and others by caring for the earth and its inhabitants.

To further connect with Ms. Richards contact: Mobile number: (592) 670-0945

E-mail: officiallandra@gmail.com

Creating Change for a Better Tomorrow Starts Today

Dr. Anana Phifer-Derilhomme 646-824-2612

CEO Founder of BlessedGirls Global World Civility Ambassador

Women & Youth Civility Practitioner International Chaplain

Talk Show Host

Facebook & LinkedIn -Anana Phifer-Derilhomme Instagram- Ananablessedgirl

YouTube-BlessedGirl TV apdfavored@gmail.com www.ananaphifer.com www.blessedgirls.com

Dr. Anana is an Entrepreneur, Talk Show Host, Author, Speaker, Success Coach, and Mentor to girls and women around the world. Most recently, Dr. Anana was appointed an International Honorary Chaplain and Coach by the Humanitarian Diplomatic Alliance. Dr. Anana was named a 2020 Iconic Influencer and featured in A Coffee Table Book Comprising Global Influencers. This book is launched in India, Switzerland, Singapore, Malaysia, Indonesia, London, and

USA. She is a Regional Stateswoman of I Change Nations. Dr. Anana Phifer-Derilhomme is the President and Founder of BlessedGirls, a Non-Profit Youth Leadership and Mentor Organization with a resourceful curriculum that educates girls and highlights female leaders from around the world to empower youth to be the change agents needed in their community to end poverty and stand for equality. BlessedGirl Academy (BGA) provides educational enrichment activities and mentoring programs designed to develop leadership skills in children considered "at risk" youth. BGA provides girls with the skills necessary to outline a life pathway that includes self-sufficiency through entrepreneurship. In order to overcome any real or perceived learning gaps all BGA activities are designed to be integrated into an existing academic environment with the cooperation of school administrators, educators, community service organizations, and other professionals while supporting the academic goals of your local schools.

BlessedGirls' most recent global campaign is the Panties and Pads Project which works to end Period Poverty in Burundi, East Africa. In 2020, BlessedGirls Global hosted 2 International Women & Youth Virtual Civility Conferences which featured female experts from the USA, South Africa, East Africa and South America. The conference highlighted challenges and provided solutions in the 4Cs: Civility, Community, Creativity and Climate Change. The 4Cs philosophy is a resource tool and reference table to assist you in your ability to improve your understanding, communication, and relationships and create a better, healthier environment for the future. It creates unity between people of all ages. The 4Cs, when used appropriately, will bridge that gap between generations, cultures and continents. Each author brings their authentic expressions, experience, and perspectives.

Dr. Anana hosts a weekly talk show and podcast, "Real Talk Real Solutions," which offers honest dialogue to produce change through civility. The podcast features world leaders, business owners and unsung heroes from around the world. The idea that one's story can inspire someone else to fulfill their purpose is what drives the dynamic talk show and its audience.

She is the recipient of The 2020 World Greatness Award in London, UK. As an International World Civility Ambassador, Dr. Anana Phifer-Derilhomme uses her wisdom and ability to direct important public issues regarding humanity and work with girls and women globally. She is the creator of the BlessedGirl Superhero - BGS (black teenage girl superhero). BGS is a cartoon character that educates, inspires and encourages girls to develop a positive self-image, business development, and community leadership. Dr. Phifer-Derilhomme is the Founder, Coach and Trainer with Moms on A Mission. MOMS Organization trains women to transform their lives with "Mission I-AM Possible" where women heal, grow, rejuvenate and stimulate their passion and fulfill their God-given purpose. The program provides proven success strategies that help others acknowledge, develop and fulfill their greatness. She is privileged to work with a team of inspiring business partners in the United States, London, Canada, South America and USVI. She is a Certified John Maxwell Coach and Trainer with proven success strategies to help you design and develop the life you dream of. Dr. Anana has provided dozens of leadership training sessions allowing attendees to reach their potential and not "postpone their purpose."

The 4C's

As a business and confidence coach she can help you get to your next BIG WIN by getting clear, confident and courageous about your purpose and destiny.

Anana is a three-time author (A Mothers Love: Letters to Our Sons, Live Your Best Life: Answer the Call, and BlessedGirl Superhero: Book of Affirmations)

She is a dedicated wife and mother to 3 extraordinary young men.

Dr. Phifer-Derilhomme is simply a blessed girl – blessed with the ability to help others discover, appreciate and manifest their blessings. She is sought-out for being an enthusiastic and accountable leader. As a professional speaker, mentored by Professor Dr. Ruben West-Black Belt Speakers Global and Prof. Ambassador Dr. Clyde Rivers, she speaks at conferences, churches, and community events about the importance of personal development, entrepreneurship, community, and self-empowerment. She has the gift and calling to get you to see past your fears and limitations, overcome your obstacles, no longer settle but SOAR into Greatness!

"As the butterfly evolves, so do we as God's chosen vessels to live a life of passion and purpose." – Dr. Anana

"People have a critique yet ignore the call to be the voice"

4Cs *Civic Lessons – people are anxious and looking for solutions.*

We are bringing the females to the front and featuring them as authors in 4Cs Creating a Better Tomorrow Starts Today (Civility, Community, Creativity & Climate Change).

You want change? Be the change.

Realizing that the future is female – it's time.

Dr. Anana has trained and mentored girls around the globe. The girls and women: over 50 in South America, 200 in East Africa, 700 in the USA, 42 in Canada. Close to one thousand women and girls have worked with Dr. Anana in either business development, personal development, civility, public speaking, or/and social justice.

The BlessedGirls Mindset – Unlimited Capacity

The BlessedGirl Economy – Develop ideas to create income and stability

The BlessedGirl Community – Work to establish programs to uplift community

BlessedGirls are created to be a blessing to others by embracing their flaws and building others around them.

BlessedGirls are free to create, activate and produce blessings everywhere they go.

You know a BlessedGirl when you see one. You know a BlessedGirl when you hear one.

You know a BlessedGirl when you read her words.

We are calling BlessedGirls from around the world to Stand UP Stand Out Stand Strong The world needs you!